Dehydrator Delights

Maximizing Flavor and Nutrition with Your Dehydrator

Andrew Overton

Copyright © 2023 - All rights reserved.

The content contained within this book may not be reproduced, duplicated, or transmitted without direct written permission from the author or the publisher.

Under no circumstances will any blame or legal responsibility be held againstthe publisher, or author, for any damages, reparation, or monetary loss due to the information contained within this book. Either directly or indirectly.

Legal Notice: This book is copyright protected. This book is only for personal use. You cannot amend, distribute, sell, use, quote, or paraphrase any part, or the content within this book, without the consent of the author or publisher.

Disclaimer Notice: Please note the information contained within this document is for educational and entertainment purposes only. All effort has been executed topresent accurate, up-to-date, and reliable, complete information. No warranties of any kind are declared or implied. Readers acknowledge that theauthor is not engaging in the rendering of legal, financial, medical, orprofessional advice. The content within this book has been derived from various sources. Please consult a licensed professional before attempting anytechniques outlined in this book.

By reading this document, the reader agrees that under no circumstances is the author responsible for any losses, direct or indirect, which are incurred as a result of the use of the information contained within this document, including, but not limited to, — errors, omissions, or inaccuracies.

Table of Contents

Dehydrating Methods

You can get started drying using items you probably already have in your kitchen.

The following items are essential to the drying process:

- Food.
- A source of heat.
- Trays or racks to dry the food on.

The trays should be slotted wood or mesh trays. Avoid using solid trays because they block air from circulating all the way around the food. In a pinch, you can cover a wood frame with cheesecloth and use it as a drying rack.

Containers to store the food in:

That's it. That's all you need to get started drying. There are other items you can use to make life easier on yourself, but the above items are the only absolute necessities.

You want to avoid trays made from the following materials because they can add harmful substances to your food during the drying process:

- Fiberglass.
- Vinyl.
- Aluminum.
- Copper.
- Plastic.
- Galvanized metal.

The following items aren't required, but will make life easier on you:

- A commercial food dehydrator.
- A fan.

- A blancher.
- A sulfur box.
- A scale.
- A thermometer.

Now that we've established the items you need and the items you can buy to make life easier, let's take a look at the various methods used to dehydrate food.

Use a fan to circulate fresh air into the area where the food is drying.

Using Your Oven

If you have an oven (and who doesn't?), you have a tool you can use to dry foods.

It isn't the best choice when it comes to drying, but it'll work in a pinch. The upside to using this method is it's one of the fastest methods of drying food. The downside is you can easily burn or scorch the food you're drying because it's difficult to keep the heat as low as you need it.

You can only dry small amounts of food in a normal kitchen oven. If you're planning on drying large amounts of food, buy a dehydrator and save yourself a lot of work.

You need to keep your oven temperature somewhere between 140 and 160 degrees F. To check oven temps, place an oven thermometer on the top rack and leave it there so you can monitor it. The temperature needs to be checked every 15 minutes to make sure it isn't getting too hot.

Place the food in a single layer on the drying trays. You can usually fit a couple pounds of food on each tray. Since most ovens have two racks, you're only going to be able to dry around 4 pounds of food at a time.

Here's a little trick you can use to fit more food in the oven: Place a couple 1 1/2-inch tall wood blocks on the bottom tray and set the next drying tray on the blocks. Then add a couple more blocks to the second tray and place another tray on it. You can fit up to four racks in your oven using this method, which will effectively double the amount of food you're able to dry at once.

Since you're not heating the oven up too hot, you don't have to worry about scorching or burning the wood.

You need to prop the door open so there's a gap of 2 to 6 inches during the drying process. If you have a fan, set it up so it's blowing air into the oven through this gap. You need to keep the air inside moving so the oven doesn't fill full of humid air.

Set your oven at its lowest temperature

If you have a gas oven, you may be able to get away with just using the heat from the pilot light. Monitor the temperature to ensure it stays above 140 degrees F and below 160 degrees F.

The top rack is going to be a little cooler than the bottom rack. Additionally, the air isn't going to be the same temperature in the front of the oven as it is in the back, especially if you're using a fan to circulate air. For this reason, it's important to rotate the trays every 20 to 30 minutes. Rotate the top trays to the bottom and flip the trays around so the food that was in the front is now in the back. You're also going to want to periodically flip your food over or stir it on the tray because the side of the food that's facing down will dry at a slower rate than the side that's facing up.

The process used to dry foods in a toaster oven is same as with a conventional oven. Place the food on a tray and put it in your toaster oven. Set the oven on its lowest setting and prop open the door. If you have a fan, use it to circulate new air into the oven.

Since this sort of oven is smaller than a conventional oven, it's going to dehydrate the food you're drying faster than the larger oven. Make sure you watch it closely and soon you'll have a small batch of dried foods.

Here's a quick tip you won't see in too many other books about drying: Open the door of your oven every few hours to let out all the damp air trapped inside. Sure, it will cause the temperature to drop inside, but it will let all the moist air inside escape, replacing it with dry air. The hit you take in temperature is temporary and it's worth it to fill the oven with fresh air.

If you only dry occasionally, your oven will do the trick nicely.

Sun-Drying

Sun-drying food is the oldest method used to dehydrate foods, predating ovens by thousands of years. This method is all-natural and doesn't require use of electricity or gas (to preserve the food or store it).

All you need is a nice, sunny day or two (or 5) in a row and you can use the power of the sun to dry your food.

In warmer climates, you can dry food using this method year-round. In cooler places or in areas where there's typically a lot of cloud cover, there may only be a handful of days a year this method can be used.

You need dry, clear weather with temperatures of at least 90 to 100 degrees F to sun-dry food.

If you live in an area where it's typically cloudy or there's a lot of moisture in the air, you're probably better off using one of the other methods of dehydrating. It's OK to move foods you've started sun-drying in and finishing the process in the oven or a dehydrator if it looks like inclement weather is on its way.

To sun-dry your foods, spread a layer out on a wood frame covered in cheesecloth. If you're worried about bugs or other animals getting to your food, you can place a layer of cheesecloth over the top of your food as well. Turn your foods regularly to assure even drying or the side left exposed to the sun will dry at a faster clip.

Alternatively, you can run a piece of string through your food items and hang them out to dry. Items like meat can be hung from hooks.

Spread food out in a single layer with at least a couple millimeters space between each piece so air can flow around it. Set the tray out in an area that gets sun for most of the day and has good circulation. Now, all you have to do is leave it there until the food is dry.

Leave the food out during the heat of the day, and then move it inside during the evening and night hours.

This accomplishes two things. It prevents the food from rehydrating due to condensation and it keeps the critters away. Animals enjoy dehydrated foods as much as you do and have been known to raid backyards at night. You don't want all of your hard work to be wasted at the hands of a marauding deer or raccoon.

Flip the food partway through each day. The bottom side gets less air and sun and will lose less moisture. Flip the food you're cooking over regularly so both side get equal amounts of sun.

There's no set time you need to leave food out to dry. All times shown in books and on the Internet are approximations of what it takes under "normal" conditions.

What exactly constitutes normal conditions is anyone's guess. What's normal in one place would be out of the ordinary somewhere else. That's probably why there's such variation in the dry times in different literature. I've tried to provide ranges in this book, but even the ranges can be off. The only way to make sure you dry your food correctly is to keep a close eye on it. When it gets close to the bottom end of the range, check it periodically.

The drying time varies based on the heat applied to the food, the humidity and the circulation of air in the area you're doing the drying. The hotter it is the faster food is going to lose moisture. The more humidity there is the slower moisture is going to be absorbed.

If you live in an area with a lot of vehicle traffic or high pollution levels, you shouldn't air-dry your food outside. Pollution particles can land on your food and contaminate it. Over time, the particulates you're eating can build up in your system and make you sick.

Dehydrating Equipment

Dehydration is mostly about prep work, so having the appropriate tools will make your job easier. Make sure you have the following tools on hand.

Baking sheet: If you don't already have one, a good-quality baking sheet that disperses heat properly and doesn't buckle under high heat is a great addition to your kitchen. Use it for roasting vegetables and fish.

Blender: Blenders are great for making purées for sauces, soups, and fruit leather. A food processor or immersion blender also works for this purpose.

Four-cup measuring pitcher: These pitchers are good for measuring liquids and for measuring the yield of dehydrated foods (if you don't have a kitchen scale).

Kitchen knife: Aside from the dehydrator itself, a kitchen knife is the most important tool for dehydrating. A good knife will make your prep work much easier. Perhaps you already have a favorite knife one that keeps a good edge, has a straight blade, and is comfortable to hold for extended periods. Good knives don't need to be expensive. In our kitchen we use the same knives many culinary schools offer; they are inexpensive but great tools for the job.

Kitchen scale: An inexpensive digital scale is very useful for measuring ingredients with precision and is also helpful for measuring and portioning the completed and dehydrated meals.

Parchment paper: Line baking sheets with parchment paper to prevent food from sticking to the pan. It also makes for easy cleanup.

How to dehydrate

Preparing Fruits for Dehydration

Most dehydrating machines, no matter which brand or model you choose, are user-friendly. The first step in preparing fruits for the dehydration machine is selecting high-quality fruits.

Fruit should be fresh and at the peak of ripeness. Once you pick or purchase your produce, thoroughly wash it and discard any bruised or damaged pieces. Fruits may need to be peeled, cored or pitted, depending on the particular fruit you are handling.

After fruit has been peeled and sliced, it is advisable to apply a pre-treatment to maintain the color and freshness of the produce. Once certain fruits, such as apples, pears and peaches are sliced, their exposure to air initiates a chemical process called oxidation that results in discolored flesh. Using an antioxidant will temporarily halt the enzyme action and prevent further damage to the texture, flavor and appearance of the fruit. To make this solution, combine a small amount of ascorbic acid (1-2 tsp.) with one cup of water and coat the fruit evenly with the liquid.

Preparing Vegetables for Dehydration

When preparing your vegetables for dehydration, be sure to select high-quality, unblemished vegetables.

Particularly for certain vegetables such as root vegetables and potatoes, make sure they are thoroughly scrubbed and cleaned prior to dehydration. Similar to fruits, vegetables should be sliced thinly and uniformly for the best results.

Nearly all vegetables should be blanched first. Blanching vegetables halts enzyme action and thereby preserves the color and flavor of the food over time some nutrients may be lost during the blanching process, place the vegetables in boiling water only for the required length of time.

After the vegetables are submerged in ice cold water, carefully dry the foods prior to placing them on trays. Note that a small number of vegetables, like mushrooms and onions, do not need to be blanched prior to dehydration.

Preparing Meat for Dehydration

Dehydrated meats are delicious and simple to prepare, but do warrant special handling instructions. Only lean meats in excellent condition should be utilized for making jerky. When using ground meat for jerky, it should be at least 93% lean.

All other meat should have its fat thoroughly trimmed prior to slicing.

You might consider applying a marinade beforehand to flavor the meat. If so, keep marinated meats in the refrigerator or freezer before placing them in the dehydrator. After removing the meat from the refrigerator, blot its surface thoroughly to remove excess moisture and place on dehydrator trays. As always, raw meat should be kept away from other foods, and all surfaces and utensils that come into contact with raw meat should be thoroughly cleaned.

After using the dehydrator, experts recommend heating dried meat strips for ten minutes in a 275° F oven or for a longer time at a lower temperature. This additional step reduces any residual chance of contamination by eliminating pathogens, and also produces the most traditional style of jerky with respect to taste and texture.

Preparing Grains, Nuts, Beans and Seeds for Dehydration

Nuts, seeds, beans and grains can all be dehydrated using a similar two-step process. First, these foods must be soaked in a water solution. Soaking deactivates anti-nutrients, stimulates nutrients such as iron, potassium and magnesium, and is beneficial to your digestive system. Soak nuts or seeds in a salt brine solution for 12-18 hours. Add ½ tsp. high-quality sea salt for every cup of water. Since wet nuts and seeds are not appealing to most people, you can place the nuts in the dehydrator to create a delicious, crunchy, ready to eat snack. After soaking for the recommended time, drain the water and proceed with instructions for your dehydrating machine.

Using Your Dehydrator Machine

Once the fruits, vegetables, herbs, meat, nuts or grains have been prepped, spread them in thin layers without overlapping on the drying trays. Turn on the dehydrating machine and set the temperature. Drying times vary depending on the dehydrator model you own and the food you are dehydrating. Most dehydrators contain guides that provide recommended temperatures and times for dehydrating specific foods.

In general, it is recommended that fruits and vegetables be dried at 130°-140° F. Meats and fish should be dehydrated at the highest temperature setting on your machine, which is typically between 145°-155° F. When dehydrating meats, it is necessary to use dehydrator models with adjustable temperature controls to ensure a product that is safe for consumption. Dried herbs require a temperature not exceeding 90° F, as aromatic oils in herbs are sensitive to high heat. Nuts, seeds and grains, which also have a high oil content, dry optimally at 90°-100° F.

Vegetables

Dehydrating fresh produce entails a little more work. These need to be rinsed, peeled, and sliced into thin layers. Some may need blanching, boiling, coring and/or de-seeding.

Always dehydrate fresh produce in a conventional oven, with temperature set between 49° / 120° and 54° / 130° only. This allows gradual loss of moisture and prevents smaller pieces from burning.

When using the dehydrator, set the machine at lowest heat for delicate vegetables (e.g. leafy vegetables, onions, etc.); and at highest heat for hardier produce (e.g. legumes, root crops, etc.) or those that have thicker cuts.

Use approximately 1½ to 2 pounds per rotation.

Artichoke hearts, green peas, freshly shelled, etc.

Blanch with hot water and then dunk into an ice bath immediately to preserve color.

Drain well. Pat-dry using paper towels, if needed.

Follow recommended steps for oven drying or dehydrating. See: Oven drying: on page 28 and Dehydrating: on page 29. These may take between five to fourteen hours. These are done when these become brittle and wrinkled.

Beets, carrots, cassava, daikon (Asian radish,) potatoes, purple carrots, purple yam, sweet potatoes, yam, zucchini.

Scrub skins well.

Except for the zucchini, parboil (partially boil) veggies until slightly fork-tender (or when you can pierce outer layer with a fork.)

Remove from water and dunk into an ice bath immediately.

When veggies are cool enough to touch, peel, and slice into ⅛-inch thick disks. Drain well. Patdry using paper towels, if needed.

Follow recommended steps for oven drying or dehydrating. See: Oven drying: on page 28 and Dehydrating: on page 29. Beets may need three to ten hours of drying. These are done when individual disks feel dry and leathery to the touch. (Important: wear food-safe gloves to prevent beet juice from staining your hands.)

Carrots, potatoes, purple yam, sweet potatoes, and yam may need six to twelve hours. While the zucchini may need five to ten hours of drying. These are done when chips become crispy. Some pieces may have air pockets or browned edges, but these are normal.

Drying Herbs and Spices

Most herbs and spices are easy to grow at home, and many can be grown in small containers on your balcony, porch or any area of your house or yard that gets regular sunlight. In addition to being a considerable way to flavor foods, herbs and spices have a number of health benefits associated with them.

Drying is the convenient way to preserve herbs and spices because all you usually have to do is lay out the leaves, flowers or seeds and let them dry and then grind or crush them as you see fit. Herbs and spices should be dried in a dehydrator because drying them in the sun can bring them to lose some of their potency.

The following herbs and spices are good candidates for drying:

- Bay
- Celery leaves
- Chervil
- Chicory
- Chives
- Cilantro
- Cinnamon sticks
- Cloves
- Dill
- Laurel
- Marjoram
- Mint
- Oregano
- Parsley
- Peppercorns
- Rosemary
- Sage
- Summer savory
- Thyme

Harvest herbs and spices by removing them from the plant in the early morning. Harvest them before the flowers open and be careful not to damage them during the harvest. Do not attempt to dry damaged pieces. The drying process isn't going to make damaged herbs and spices any better.

Lay the herbs or spices out in a single layer on the dehydrator tray and spread them out so there's a bit of space between them for air circulation. Most herbs and spices should be dried at temperatures between 115 and 125 degrees F, but be assured to check the documentation that came with your dehydrator to see what the recommended temperature for drying herbs and spices is.

The drying time for herbs and spices should be short. Most herbs and spices should be done drying in less than 4 hours. Herbs and spices are done when they feel crispy and are brittle to the touch. You should be able to crumble leaves, stems and flowers between your fingers.

Some herbs and spices can be hung out to air dry. Rosemary, thyme, sage and parsley can all be hung inside the house and left to dry. Basil, oregano and mint leaves need to be placed inside a paper bag before being hung out to dry. Air-drying can be done indoors or out, but be sure to hang the herbs and spices in a shaded area if drying them outside. Air-drying herbs by hanging them can take a week or two to properly dry the herbs.

Herbs and some spices can be dried in the microwave if you're in a hurry. Microwave them on high for 2 minutes and check them. If they're still wet, microwave them for 30 seconds and check them again. Continue microwaving the herbs in 30-second increments until they're done drying.

Storing Herbs and Spices

Here's the dilemma. Herbs and spices will last a lot longer when they're left whole, but they're usually ground or crushed when they're used in recipes. It's kind of a hassle to grind or crush your herbs every time you want to use them, especially when you're looking to make a quick meal.

What I do is dry a large batch of herbs and spices. I crush up half of it and store it that way, so I always have crushed or ground herbs and spices on hand. I then store the rest of it in the freezer whole. When I start to run low, I crush or grind the herbs I have in the freezer and I'm ready to go. I know when I pull a batch out of the freezer, I'm going to need to dry more soon or I'm going to run out.

Are nutrients lost during drying?

There are some nutrients lost during pretreatment and drying. Any time the food is exposed to heat, light or oxygen, there will be some degradation of nutritional value. The longer the exposure, the greater the damage. Most fruits start degrading as soon as they're harvested. This degradation is sped up by cutting into them or otherwise exposing the flesh to oxygen.

Many fruits contain enzymes that react to the air and cause browning and nutrient loss to begin as soon as they're cut into. If you've ever left an apple or a banana out for a while and seen it turn brown, you've seen these enzymes in action. This reaction to the oxygen in the air can be slowed to a crawl by pretreating or blanching the fruit after it's been cut.

The following vitamins can be damaged by too much heat, light or air exposure:

- Folate (heat)
- Riboflavin (heat)
- Thiamine (heat, light)
- Vitamin A (air, light)
- Vitamin B12 (heat, light)

Commercial foods that undergo intense treatment lose a lot more nutrients than fruit dried at home. While commercially dried foods can lose up to 80% of certain vitamins, foods dried at home usually don't come anywhere near that magnitude.

Take the following precautions to reduce the amount of vitamins lost while treating and drying produce:

Work on small batches of food at a time.

When you work on large batches and try to get a lot of fruit done at once, the pieces you cut into first are left to sit out while you process the rest of the produce. This can result in the earlier pieces degrading a lot faster than those cut later on.

Move food into pretreatment shortly after it's been cut.

Time is of essence when treating fruit that's prone to discoloration. It's important to slow down enzymatic reactions as early as possible to avoid nutrient loss.

Carefully regulate heat.

High heat can accelerate nutrient loss, so its important heat is monitored closely. Using a dehydrator allows you the most control over the amount of heat drying food is exposed to. Blanching also exposes food to heat and can damage nutrients, but may be critical to ensuring food can be properly stored. Blanching isn't as critical of a process with fruit as it is with vegetables.

Store dried food in an airtight container.

This will minimize the amount of air the food comes in contact with. If air is allowed into the container, the food can take up moisture from the air, drastically shortening how long the food will last.

Drying food in the sun exposes it to UV rays that can damage light-sensitive vitamins.

When vitamin retention is of concern, a dehydrator may be the better choice for drying.

Store food in small, single-serving containers.

Every time you open a container, more air is let in. Using single serving containers only exposes the food you plan on eating to new air.

No minerals are lost during the drying process, but pretreatment can cause some mineral loss. Boiling or otherwise exposing fruit to water may cause some of the minerals to leach out into the water. This can happen during blanching and again during rehydration. The drying process itself doesn't affect minerals.

Calories and sugar are largely unaffected by the drying process, but they will be concentrated into a smaller package. A raisin has the same caloric content and amount of sugar as it did when it was a grape, but it's now packed into the smaller raisin. Dried produce has more calories and more sugar than regular produce when compared by volume. For example, 100 grams of grapes have 15 grams of sugar and 70 calories. 100 grams of raisins have 60 grams of sugar and 300 calories. Raisins have 3 times the sugar and more than 4 times the calories than grapes when compared by volume.

For this reason, it's important not to overeat when it comes to dried fruit and vegetables. They can be a healthy part of most diets, but only if consumed in moderation.

The Best Techniques to Preserve Dried Foods

Over drying the dried food is just impossibility. So, when you are unsure if the food is completely dry or not, keeps drying it until you are entirely sure.

Never use granulated sugar in fruit leathers as the sugar will get crystallize over time. You can opt for honey or corn syrup if you need.

To be considered "dehydrated," foods must be at least 95% moisture-free. If they aren't and you try to store them, they'll quickly rot. How can you tell? If the food is soft, spongy, and sticky, it's back in the dehydrator they go. You can't really "over dry" food, so the harder and crunchier, the better. If you don't want certain foods to be that dry, you'll have to plan on eating them pretty much right away before bacteria has a chance to get at that moisture.

Store food properly

The last step you need to remember in the dehydration process is safe storage. All food should be stored in clean and dry containers, with airtight lids that can keep out moisture and bugs. If you're a prepper and don't plan on snacking frequently on your dehydrated foods just yet, vacuum-sealing is a great option.

Safe storage also means knowing how long a food is going to last, because even the most dehydrated food doesn't last forever. The only exception is freeze-dried foods, which can last decades, but most people don't have a special freeze-drier machine. Bear in mind that storebought dehydrated foods last longer than homemade ones, because of the added preservatives. As an example, jerky you buy at the store lasts about a year, while home-dehydrated will only last 1-2 months when properly stored.

Health food stores usually stock bulk items such as rice, flour, pasta, millet, etc. Ask if you can buy them in bulk. Many stores will usually give a discount for whole case or whole bag purchases.

You will still have to store them in a bucket or some other container. You can use whatever food containers you have. Just make sure they were not used for toxic or hazardous materials. You don't want toxic residues to contaminate your food.

If you want, you can store your bulk items in plastic food storage bags available in any grocery store. The one-gallon and two-gallon sizes work well for this purpose. Squeeze the air out of the bag before sealing it. You can also add oxygen absorber packets before

After sealing the plastic bag, you can add an extra layer of protection by wrapping it with aluminum foil. This will act as a light bather. Then put this in another larger plastic bag, squeeze the air out and seal.

Mylar Bags (Metalized Liners)

To seal these bags, you can use foil tape. One brand is Refectix and should be available in hardware stores. If not, check with plumbing supply stores. A 30-foot roll costs around $4. If there is still air in the bag after you seal it, prick a little hole in it and push the air out. Then seal up the hole. Or you can use a portable heat sealer which can cost over 100 dollars.

If you don't want to use food buckets, you can store these packages in cardboard boxes – just make sure you have no mice. Or you can use the 18 gallon and 22 gallon storage tote containers sold just about anywhere (Wal-Mart, Kmart, Pamida, Gibson, hardware stores). Rubbermaid makes them as well as other companies. They cost around $5 to $7 each.

If there is a food service (restaurant) supplies store near you, go and see what is available that you can use.

The dryer the food is, the longer it can be stored for, so you'll want as much moisture in the food to be removed as possible. Airtight plastic bags and/or containers are great options for holding the food and resisting spoilage. Most of the nutritional value in dehydrated foods will be preserved, although it won't be as nutritious as it would be otherwise.

Remember that when storing any food for the long term, the food needs to be stored in a cool and dry location at room temperature. Any location that's humid or excessively hot should be automatically rejected for storing food because the food will be more likely to mold, even if it's been preserved.

How to Store Jerky

The best way to store jerky is to treat it like a fresh food item.

Limit the jerky's exposure to air.

Retain the quality of your jerky by placing it in an airtight container. Vacuum packing, sealable bags and plastic wrap can be used to wrap your jerky and are effective at keeping air out. The option that would allow the jerky to be most easily accessible is to place it in a storage container or jar that has a lid.

Label the container with the date at the beginning of the storage life so you know the age of the jerky and how long it has been stored.

Separate your jerky by type. Place different types of jerky in different containers to keep the flavors separate, ensuring top quality.

Eradicate any source of moisture.

Use a paper towel to dry your jerky. If you notice moisture or oil on your jerky, noted by wetness or a sheen on the surface, gently pat the surfaces of the meat with a paper towel.

Keep moisture at bay while the jerky is in storage by placing the jerky between layers of paper towel in the container. The towels will absorb any moisture from the jerky or container. Replace the towels when you notice any presence of moisture.

Know the shelf life of your jerky.

Time will take a toll on the quality of your jerky. With proper storage techniques, jerky can safely be stored for varying lengths of time depending on where you choose to store it.

Leave your jerky in a cool, dry place. When placed properly in an airtight container, you can leave your jerky on the counter top or another cool, dry place for no longer than 1 month.

Put your jerky in the refrigerator. Jerky can be stored in the refrigerator to be used within 6 months.

Store homemade jerky in the freezer. Jerky lasts up to 1-year when kept in your freezer

How to Store Herbs?

When completely dry, separate the leaves from the stems, and store the leaves (either whole or gently crumbled) in light-proof containers.

In terms of oven-drying, allow the dried herbs to cool, and gently crush the leaves. Store the dried herbs in light-proof containers.

Store all your dried herbs in a cool dark place, in airtight containers.

Never store your herb vinegars in the sun or on a lighted counter if you intend to use them, no matter how pretty they look. They should always be stored in the refrigerator.

FAQS

How long will dehydrated food last?

If prepared and stored properly, dehydrated food is can last 5 to 10 years. But it is advisable to use your own within four to six months.

Does dehydrating food remove (or preserve) nutrients?

Yes, some nutrients may be removed when food is dehydrated but no more than other methods of preservation. Heat and light are responsible for the breakdown of vitamins. By implication, the canning method of preservation tears down more nutrients than the low heat, low moisture dehydrating method. The amount of thiamin and vitamin A & C that diminishes from your vegetables can be reduced through blanching.

Does dehydrating food kill bacteria?

Provided that you dehydrate your vegetables and fruits until their moisture levels are anywhere between five and twenty percent, you have removed the bacteria that can cause food to decay. If you are concern about bacteria on meat, it is recommended by the USDA that you first heat your raw meat to 160°F temperature and then dehydrate at a steady temperature of 145°F.

Does Dehydrate Food Increase Sugar?

In most cases, yes, because when you dehydrate food at a higher temperate, it will cause the death of enzymes. More dense foods may withstand higher temperatures without the enzymes being killed. But most enzymes will ultimately become dormant when the temperature rises between 140° to 160°F.

Can Cooked Food Be Dehydrated?

Yes. Meals can even be dehydrated, but some cooked food dehydrates better than others. If you are drying food for long-term storage, camping, or backpacking, you can prepare rice dishes, stews, and desserts and dry them by using nonstick sheets on the trays of dehydrator. And then remove the nonstick sheet when they have reached a moist, crumbly consistency.

How can I store dried food?

Dehydrated vegetables can last up to ten years and fruit up to five if properly stored. The best way to preserve your dried food for the long term is to vacuum seal using an oxygen absorber and keep it in a cool, dark place. If you are going to eat non-meat dried food within 12 months, store them in reusable storage bags or freezer bags with the air squeezed out.

If you will consume seafood and meat within a month, you can store in freezer bags and keep them in a cool, dark place; otherwise, the best thing is to vacuum seal and freeze them. Meat can last for up to a year if properly stored in the freezer.

The Best Ways, Temperature and Cooking Times to Dry Foods

Ways at Home

Pre-treating food

For best results, most of the food items need to be pre-treated before dehydration. Following are the commonly used pre-treatments:

Ascorbic acid or Vitamin C bath

By soaking fruits or soft vegetables in an ascorbic acid solution (one-part of ascorbic acid in 1 gallon of water) immediately after cutting will stop discoloring and browning. An exception is leafy greens, herbs, and broccoli as the acid will discolor them severely. For this, soak the cut fruits immediately in the solution for 8 to 10 minutes. Drain for dehydration.

Skin cracking

Fruits with tougher skins such as plums, cherries, grapes, figs, or berries may need their skins to be cracked before dehydration to pull moisture out from the fruit properly. For this, boil a pot of water and dip the fruit in it for 15 seconds. Remove and dip them in ice-cold water immediately. Drain water entirely before drying them.

Blanching

It is a process used for scalding vegetables in boiling water or steam, to stop the enzymatic action within the vegetables. Be cautious about the timing, as over blanching results in loss of nutrients and under blanching can cause food spoilage during or after the dehydration. For blanching, usually, two methods are used: boiling vegetables in water for some time, and scalding vegetables above the boiling water level, also known as steam blanching — steam from the boiling water scalds the vegetables.

Citric Acid bath

Citric Acid kills bacteria and stops food discolouration. For this, mix a teaspoon of citric acid in 2.5 cups of water, or you can mix equal parts of water and lemon juice. Soak the food for 8 to 10 minutes and drain entirely before dehydration.

Storage

Dehydrated foods can last for years if stored properly. To ensure maximum shelf life, you need to prevent dried food from moisture, heat, microorganism, light and oxygen. Essential steps of storage are:

Cooling

When the fruit is dry enough, remove it from the dehydrator and cool the fruit completely in a cool and dry place for half an hour; storing warm food will reintroduce moisture due to condensation. Make sure not to leave the dried food for too long as it will also result in moisture to come back into the food.

Conditioning

To ensure even distribution of moisture within the food, place the dried food in loose packaging and seal it for 2 to 4 days.

Packaging

As a final step of storage, you need to pack your dehydrated food in air-tight jars or cans. Store your jars or containers in a cool, dark, and dry place to maximise the shelf-life.

Types of Dehydrators

Although there are many methods to dehydrate food such as sun drying and oven drying, the most convenient method is by using an electric dehydrator. Why?

Because it is an easy and hassle-free way to dehydrate your food.

You can get commercial electrical dehydrators from the market that matches your needs, or you can go for DIY dehydrator at home.

DIY home dehydrator

You can construct your dehydrator, if you need to produce large batches of dried foods, from a wooden framed box. All you need is constant heat (gas burner) and airflow (a fan) and few shelves or trays to put food on. However, it becomes difficult to control the temperature levels if you are a beginner, and sometimes it results in a complete mess due to a complicated cleaning process. You need a lot of experimentation and testing to achieve the optimum temperature levels in DIY dehydrators.

Electric dehydrators

If you plan to dry your food regularly, then investing in a commercial electrical dehydrator is the best option. They can handle large quantities of food, and the best part is, you can control the temperature and air circulation without putting much effort. In a useful and well-made electric dehydrator, the temperature remains constant throughout the drying process with the help of a thermostatically-controlled heating system, and proper airflow is achieved through a built-in fan to ensure complete evaporation.

You can get a small unit with 4 or 5 trays under a hundred dollars if you want to dry small batches in one go. However, if you intend to dry a lot of food at once, you can get a commercial dehydrator with ten trays or more.

Dehydration Tool Kit

You have bought a good and suitable dehydrator, but there are still some other tools and products you may need to increase the productivity and the quality of your dried food. But remember to keep them simple and easy to use. You would need:

- Apple peeler and cherry pitter for quick and efficient work
- You will need a deep container with a tight lid for blanching
- A colander to fit into the container to hold food items for blanching
- Stainless steel knives for cutting food and meat
- Ascorbic acid or lemon juice to give Vitamin C bath to fruits
- Large pot or tub to hold Ascorbic Acid or lemon juice solution
- A blender to make fruit leathers, or to powder your dehydrated food
- Disposable latex or vinyl gloves to handle dried foods to prevent spoilage as handling dried foods with hands transform moisture and heat from your hands to the food.
- Nylon mesh to place on trays or shelves
- Air-tight containers for storing dehydrated foods such as mason jars or cans with air-tight lids, or zip lock bags that can be vacuum-sealed.
- A food processor for grating and slicing vegetables evenly
- A meat slicer to cut the meat evenly in desired thickness quickly and efficiently, and for slicing the fruits and vegetables evenly for making chips and crackers.
- Sometimes you need to soak and spray the food with vitamin C or lemon juice before dehydrating to avoid browning. For this, a spray bottle is a mess-free option and do the work quickly.
- For making leathers, a squeeze bottle is quite useful. You can

squeeze the puree out straight onto drying sheets, or you can even mix different colored purees to form a multicolored design.

Using a dehydrator is the most effective way to remove moisture from food and extend its shelflife.

Dehydrator-drying

Dehydrating with a food dehydrator is the best method these days. You have control over temperature, time, and air flow. You place food on a tray, close the lid, and heat at the appropriate temperature with an electrical heating element for the given time. Times vary depending on what you're drying and how much. A fan circulates heat around the food, while vents allow the moist air to escape.

Quality

Any appliance that touches food should meet certain standards. Add heat, and the possibility of food becoming contaminated with chemicals, and the quality of materials becomes a big issue. Dehydrator trays are made of plastic, so you want to check if they're BPA-free if it's a concern for you. With better materials comes a higher price tag, but that isn't the primary driver of cost.

You can still find affordable dehydrators made from relatively chemical-free parts.

Vegetables

Maple carrot straws

Preparation time: 15 minutes | Dehydration time: 6 hours | Servings: 4

Ingredients:

- 1 lb. Carrots, sliced into long strips
- 1 tablespoon maple syrup
- 1 tablespoon olive oil
- Salt to taste

Direction:

1. Combine all the ingredients in a bowl.
2. Arrange the strips in the cosori premium food dehydrator.
3. Process at 135 degrees f for 6 hours.
4. Storage suggestions: store in a food container.

Tip: use a peeler to slice the carrots.

Nutrition Calories: 214 Fat 3 g Carbs 41.4 g Protein 4.3 g

Dehydrated asparagus

Preparation time: 10 minutes | Dehydration time: 6 hours | Servings: 2

Ingredients:

- 4 cups asparagus, trimmed and sliced

Direction:

1. Arrange the asparagus in the cosori premium food dehydrator.
2. Process at 125 degrees f for 6 hours.
3. Storage suggestions: store in a sealable plastic bag.

Tip: you can also season the asparagus with salt or garlic powder.

Nutrition Calories: 434 Fat 39.4 g Carbs 20.9 g Protein 5.8 g

Fall carrot chips

Preparation time: 15 minutes | Dehydration time: 6 hours | Servings: 4

Ingredients:

- 1 pound of carrots, peeled
- 3 tbsp. Melted coconut oil
- 3/4 tsp. Salt
- 2 tsp. Allspice (or combination of cinnamon, allspice or nutmeg)

Direction:

1. Wash, dry and slice carrots into uniform disks.
2. Mix together carrots, oil, salt and allspice.
3. Place carrots onto dehydrator trays and dry for 6-6 hours at 125 degrees or until crisp.

Nutrition Calories::11, sodium: 337 mg, dietary fiber: 0.7 g, total fat: 0 g, total carbs: 2.7 g, protein: 0.2 g.

Herbed sweet potato chips

Preparation time: 15 minutes | Dehydration time: 6 hours | Servings: 4

Ingredients:

- 3 medium to large sweet potatoes
- 4 tbsp. Olive oil
- 2 tbsp. Fresh lemon juice
- 2 tsp. Dried thyme
- 1 1/2 tsp. Salt
- 1/4 tsp. Pepper

Direction:

1. Slice sweet potatoes into thin, uniform slices.

2. In a bowl combine sweet potato slices, oil, lemon juice, thyme, salt and pepper. Toss until well coated.
3. Place slices on dehydrator trays.
4. Set the temperature to 140 degrees. Dehydrate for 6-6 hours, or until crisp to touch.

Nutrition Calories: 35, sodium: 721 mg, dietary fiber: 1.9 g, total fat: 0.2 g, total carbs: 8.3 g, protein: 0.6 g.

☆ ☆ ☆ ☆ ☆

Dried cauliflower popcorn

Preparation time: 15 minutes | Dehydration time: 8 hours | Serving: 1

Ingredients:

- 2 cups cauliflower florets
- 4 tablespoons hot sauce
- 3 tablespoons coconut oil
- 1 teaspoon smoked cayenne
- 1/2 teaspoon ground cumin
- 1 tablespoons paprika

Direction:

1. Toss the cauliflower florets in hot sauce and coconut oil.
2. Sprinkle with the smoked cayenne, cumin and paprika.
3. Add the seasoned cauliflower to the cosori premium food dehydrator.
4. Dry at 130 degrees f for 8 hours.
5. Storage suggestions: store in an airtight plastic bag.

Tip: add more cayenne pepper for spicier cauliflower popcorn.

Nutrition Calories:: 9, sodium: 0 mg, dietary fiber: 0 g, total fat: 0 g, total carbs: 2.1 g, protein:0.2 g.

☆ ☆ ☆ ☆ ☆

Zucchini snacks

Preparation time: 45 minutes | Dehydration time: 12 hours | Servings: 4

Ingredients:

- 8 zucchinis, sliced into rounds and seeds removed
- 1 cup grape juice concentrate
- 1 cup water

Direction:

1. Add all the ingredients to a pot over medium heat.
2. Bring to a boil.
3. Reduce heat and simmer for 30 minutes.
4. Drain the zucchini and let cool.
5. Add the zucchinis to the cosori premium food dehydrator.
6. Process at 135 degrees f for 12 hours.
7. Storage suggestions: store in the refrigerator for up to 1 week.

Tip: do not overcook the zucchinis.

Nutrition Calories:: 9, sodium: 0 mg, dietary fiber: 0 g, total fat: 0 g, total carbs: 2.1 g, protein: 0.2 g.

Cucumber chips

Preparation time: 15 minutes | Dehydration time: 6 hours | Servings: 4

Ingredients:

- 3 cucumber, sliced into rounds
- 1 tablespoon avocado oil
- 2 teaspoons apple cider vinegar
- Salt to taste

Direction:

1. Toss the cucumber slices in avocado oil and vinegar.

2. Season with the salt.
3. Add the cucumber slices to the cosori premium food dehydrator.
4. Dehydrate at 135 degrees f for 6 hours.
5. Storage suggestions: store in an airtight container.

Tip: you can use a mandoline slicer to slice the cucumbers thinly. Dry the cucumber slices with a paper towel before processing.

Nutrition Calories:: 9, sodium: 0 mg, dietary fiber: 0 g, total fat: 0 g, total carbs: 2.1 g, protein: 0.2 g.

Dehydrated okra

Preparation time: 15 minutes | Dehydration time: 12 hours | Servings: 4

Ingredients:

- 12 okra, sliced

Direction:

1. Add the okra to the cosori premium food dehydrator.
2. Dry at 130 degrees f for 12 hours.
3. Storage suggestions: store in an airtight container.

Tip: sprinkle with powdered herb or spice for added flavor.

Nutrition: calories 70, fat 4, fiber 4, carbs 30, protein 2

Dried sweet potato

Preparation time: 10 minutes | Dehydration time: 12 hours | Servings: 4

Ingredients:

- 2 sweet potatoes

- 1 teaspoon onion powder

Direction:

1. Season the sweet potato slices with onion powder.
2. Arrange in a single layer in the cosori premium food dehydrator.
3. Set at 115 degrees f.
4. Process for 12 hours.
5. Storage suggestions: store in a sealable plastic bag.

Tip: use a mandolin slicer to prepare the sweet potatoes.

Nutrition: calories 70, fat 4, fiber 4, carbs 30, protein 2

Dehydrated beets

Preparation time: 20 minutes | Dehydration time: 12 hours | Servings: 4

Ingredients:

- 3 beets, sliced thinly
- 1/4 cup water
- 1/4 cup vinegar
- 1 tablespoon olive oil
- Salt to taste

Direction:

1. Combine all the ingredients in a bowl.
2. Marinate for 10 minutes.
3. Arrange the beet slices in the cosori premium food dehydrator.
4. Dehydrate at 135 degrees f for 12 hours.
5. Storage suggestions: store in a sealable plastic bag.

Tip: use a mandoliner slicer to slice the beets thinly.

Nutrition: calories 70, fat 4, fiber 4, carbs 30, protein 2

☆ ☆ ☆ ☆ ☆

Dehydrated tomatoes

Preparation time: 20 minutes | Dehydration time: 8 hours | Servings: 2

Ingredients:

- 2 tomatoes, sliced into quarters
- Salt to taste

Direction:

1. Add the tomatoes to the cosori premium food dehydrator.
2. Sprinkle with salt.
3. Set to 135 degrees f.
4. Process for 8 hours.
5. Storage suggestions: store in a sealable plastic bag.
6. Squeeze out the air. Store for up to 2 months in a cool dry place.
7. Freeze and store for up to 6 months.

Tip: don't forget to scrape the seeds before drying.

Nutrition Calories: 250 Fat 7.6 g Carbs 41.8 g Protein 4.5 g

☆ ☆ ☆ ☆ ☆

Spiced cucumbers

Preparation time: 20 hours | Dehydration time: 4 hours | Servings: 2

Ingredients:

- 2 cucumbers, sliced into rounds
- 2 teaspoons olive oil
- 2 teaspoons vinegar
- 1tablespoon paprika
- 2 teaspoons onion powder

- 2 teaspoons garlic powder
- 2 teaspoons sugar
- Pinch chili powder

Direction:

1. Toss the cucumbers in oil and vinegar.
2. Sprinkle with the sugar and spices.
3. Put the cucumber slices in the cosori premium food dehydrator.
4. Process at 135 degrees f for 6 hours.
5. Storage suggestions: store in an airtight container.

Tip: dehydrate longer if you want your cucumber crispier.

Nutrition Calories: 250 Fat 7.6 g Carbs 41.8 g Protein 4.5 g

☆ ☆ ☆ ☆ ☆

Dehydrated corn

Preparation time: 10 minutes | Dehydration time: 12 hours | Servings: 4

Ingredients:

- 8 cups corn kernels

Direction:

1. Spread the corn kernels in the cosori premium food dehydrator.
2. Process at 125 degrees f for 12 hours.
3. Storage suggestions: store in a glass jar with lid.

Tip: you can also drizzle the corn kernels in olive oil before dehydrating.

Nutrition Calories: 214 Fat 3 g Carbs 41.4 g Protein 4.3 g

☆ ☆ ☆ ☆ ☆

Hot & spicy potato sticks

Preparation time: 15 minutes | Dehydration time: 6 hours | Servings: 4

Ingredients:

- 2 large idaho potatoes, peeled and cut like french fries
- 3-4 tsp. Olive oil
- 1/2 tsp. Cumin
- 1/4 tsp. Black pepper
- 1/4 tsp. Cayenne pepper (or more for increased spiciness)
- Dash of hot pepper sauce
- Salt to taste

Direction:

1. Blanch potatoes in a pot of boiling water for 4-6 minutes.
2. Transfer potatoes to a bowl of ice water.
3. Combine potatoes, olive oil, cumin, both peppers and hot pepper sauce.
4. Lay potatoes onto dehydrator trays.
5. Set the dehydrator to 135 degrees and dehydrate for 8-6 hours.

Nutrition Calories: 5, sodium: 1 mg, dietary fiber: 0 g, total fat: 0.1 g, total carbs: 1 g, protein: 0.1 g.

Indian cauliflower

Preparation time: 15 minutes | Dehydration time: 6 hours | Servings: 4

Ingredients:

- 2 heads cauliflower, cut into bite size pieces
- 1/4 cup low sodium soy sauce
- 1/8 cup honey
- 1 tsp. Curry powder

- 1 tsp. Turmeric

Direction:

1. Blend all ingredients in a bowl except cauliflower. Whisk to ensure honey is incorporated. Add cauliflower and mix well so vegetables are well coated.
2. Place cauliflower pieces onto dehydrator sheets and dehydrate at 140 degrees for one hour. Lower the temperature and dehydrate at 110 degrees for another 6 hours or until crispy.

Nutrition Calories: 20, sodium: 8 mg, dietary fiber: 0.9 g, total fat: 0.2 g, total carbs: 4.7 g, protein: 0.6 g.

Lemon pepper yellow squash rounds

Preparation time: 15 minutes | Dehydration time: 6 hours | Servings: 4

Ingredients:

- 2 large yellow squash, cut into 1/8" thick rounds
- 3-4 tsp. Olive oil
- 1 tbsp. Lemon juice
- 1/2 tsp. Lemon pepper seasoning
- Salt to taste

Direction:

1. Toss squash slices with olive oil until well coated. Add lemon juice, lemon pepper seasoning and salt and combine all ingredients thoroughly.
2. Spread squash onto dehydrator trays.
3. Set the dehydrator to 135 degrees and dehydrate for 10-12 hours. Halfway through, flip each chip over to prevent sticking.

Nutrition Calories:: 5, sodium: 3 mg, dietary fiber: 0 g, total fat: 0.1

g, total carbs: 0.9 g, protein: 0.3 g.

Smoked collard green chips

Preparation time: 15 minutes | Dehydration time: 6 hours | Servings: 4

Ingredients:

- 1 bunch collard greens, washed and leaves roughly torn
- 3 tbsp. Olive oil
- 1/2 tsp. Smoked paprika
- 1/2 tsp. Sea salt
- 1/4 tsp. Pepper

Direction:

1. Toss collard greens, olive oil and spices in a bowl.
2. Place collard greens onto a dehydrator tray.
3. Set the temperature to 140 degrees. Dehydrate for 2-4 hours, or until crispy.

Nutrition Calories:: 16, sodium: 262 mg, dietary fiber: 0.7 g, total fat: 0.1 g, total carbs: 3.4 g, protein: 0.9 g.

Smoky sweet potato chips

Preparation time: 15 minutes | Dehydration time: 6 hours | Servings: 4

Ingredients:

- 3 large sweet potatoes, washed and sliced into very thin slices
- 2 tsp. Olive oil
- 1 1/2 tsp. Smoked paprika
- Sea salt to taste

Direction:

1. Blanch potatoes in a pot of boiling water for 4-6 minutes.
2. Transfer potatoes to a bowl of ice water.
3. Combine sliced potatoes, olive oil, smoked paprika and salt.
4. Lay potatoes onto dehydrator trays.
5. Set the dehydrator to 135 degrees and dehydrate for 8-6 hours, or until crispy.

Nutrition Calories:: 37, sodium: 3 mg, dietary fiber: 1.8 g, total fat: 0.3 g, total carbs: 8.5 g, protein: 0.7 g.

Spinach balls

Preparation time: 15 minutes | Dehydration time: 6 hours | Servings: 4

Ingredients:

- 3 cups cashews
- 3 cups blanched spinach
- 4 tbsp. Olive oil
- 1/4 cup dehydrated onion flakes
- 3 cloves of garlic
- 1/4 tsp. Nutmeg
- Pinch of cayenne pepper

Direction:

1. Process the cashews until they are finely ground. Add all the remaining ingredients and pulse several times until well combined and paste-like in consistency.
2. Pour mixture into a bowl and form into small, bite-size balls.
3. Place spinach balls on dehydrator sheets and dehydrate at 120 degrees for 5 hours.

Nutrition Calories:: 137, sodium: 7 mg, dietary fiber: 0.9 g, total fat: 10.5 g, total carbs: 9.2 g, protein: 3.7 g.

★ ★ ★ ★ ☆

Sour cream and onion potato chips

Preparation time: 15 minutes | Dehydration time: 6 hours | Servings: 4

Ingredients:

- 2 large russet potatoes, washed, peeled and sliced into chunks
- 1/2 cup sour cream
- 1 1/2 cups water
- 1 tbsp. Onion powder
- 1 tbsp. Minced onion
- 1 tbsp. Dried parsley
- 1 1/2 tsp. Salt
- 1/2 tsp. Black pepper

Direction:

1. Cook potatoes in a pot of boiling water until soft.
2. Drain potatoes when done and place in a bowl with the remaining ingredients.
3. Use an immersion blender to create a soft paste.
4. Use a spatula to smooth the paste onto the dehydrator sheets in a fairly thin layer.
5. Set the dehydrator to 145 degrees. Place trays in dehydrator for 4-6 hours. Flip and return to the dehydrator for several hours, for a total of 9-6 hours.
6. Once cooled, break into smaller pieces.

Nutrition Calories: 40, sodium: 505 mg, dietary fiber: 0.6 g, total fat: 2.2 g, total carbs: 4.7 g, protein: 0.9 g.

★ ★ ★ ★ ☆

Southwestern style cauliflower popcorn

Preparation time: 15 minutes | Dehydration time: 6 hours | Servings: 4

Ingredients:

- 1 head cauliflower, cut into bite sized pieces
- 1 tsp. Paprika
- 1 tsp. Oregano
- 1 tsp. Coriander
- 1 tsp. Cumin
- 1/4 tsp. Onion powder
- 1/4 tsp. Garlic powder
- 1/8 – 1/4 tsp. Cayenne pepper
- 1/2 tsp. Salt
- 3 tbsp. Olive oil

Direction:

1. Blend all the seasonings and olive oil in a bowl. Add cauliflower and combine to coat all the florets.
2. Place cauliflower pieces onto dehydrator sheets and dehydrate at 140 degrees for one hour. Lower the temperature and dehydrate at 110 degrees for another 6 hours or until crispy.

Nutrition Calories: 17, sodium: 212 mg, dietary fiber: 1.6 g, total fat: 0.5 g, total carbs: 3.1 g, protein: 1 g.

Marinated eggplant

Preparation time: 15 minutes | Dehydration time: 6 hours | Servings: 4

Ingredients:

- 1 eggplant, peeled or unpeeled
- 1/4 cup olive oil
- 4 tbsp. Balsamic vinegar

- 2 tbsp. Maple syrup
- 1/2 tsp. Sriracha sauce
- Salt and pepper to taste

Direction:

1. Slice eggplant into long, uniform strips.
2. Combine oil, vinegar, maple syrup and srircaha sauce with eggplant in a bowl. Sprinkle on salt and pepper to taste. Refrigerate for a minimum of 2 hours.
3. Place eggplant on dehydrator trays and dehydrate for 12-18 hours at 115 degrees.

Nutrition Calories:: 17, sodium: 7 mg, dietary fiber: 0.8 g, total fat: 0.1 g, total carbs: 4.3 g, protein: 0.2 g.

Mediterranean style "sun-dried" tomatoes

Preparation time: 15 minutes | Dehydration time: 6 hours | Servings: 4

Ingredients:

- 4 large firm, ripe tomatoes
- 1 1/2 tsp. Mixed dried herbs, such as oregano, thyme and basil
- 1/2 tsp. Sea salt

Direction:

1. Wash tomatoes and cut off tops. Tomatoes do not need to peeled and seeded. Slice tomatoes into ¼ inch thick slices.
2. Sprinkle tomatoes with herbs and salt and place on dehydrator trays.
3. Set the dehydrator to 145 degrees and dehydrate for 8-6 hours, or until leathery.

Nutrition Calories:: 5, sodium: 325 mg, dietary fiber: 0 g, total fat:

0.1 g, total carbs: 1.1 g, protein: 0.2 g.

Moroccan carrot crunch

Preparation time: 15 minutes | Dehydration time: 6 hours | Servings: 4

Ingredients:

- 1 pound of carrots, peeled
- 4 tbsp. Olive oil
- 1 tbsp. Honey
- 1/8 tsp. Cayenne pepper
- 2 tsp. Cumin
- 1 tsp. Dried parsley flakes
- 1/2 tsp. Salt

Direction:

1. Wash, dry and thinly slice carrots.
2. Mix together oil, honey, and seasonings.
3. Place carrots onto dehydrator trays. Using a pastry brush, dab the mixture onto the carrot rounds.
4. Dehydrate for 6-6 hours at 125 degrees or until crisp.

Nutrition Calories: 26, sodium: 262 mg, dietary fiber: 0.7 g, total fat: 0.3 g, total carbs: 6 g, protein: 0.5 g

Parmesan cucumber chips

Preparation time: 15 minutes | Dehydration time: 6 hours | Servings: 4

Ingredients:

- 5 cups cucumber slices, thinly sliced with a mandolin

- 2 tbsp. Olive oil
- 1/2 tsp. Salt
- 1/4 tsp. Black pepper
- 1/2 tsp. Dried parsley flakes
- 1/2 cup freshly grated parmesan cheese

Direction:

1. Mix the salt, pepper, parsley flakes and parmesan cheese in a bowl. Toss sliced cucumbers with olive oil and combine with seasoning and cheese mixture. Coat the slices well.
2. Place slices on dehydrator sheets and dehydrate for 8-6 hours at 135 degrees.

Nutrition Calories:: 39, sodium: 220 mg, dietary fiber: 0 g, total fat: 2.4 g, total carbs: 1.1 g, protein: 3.7 g.

Ranch brussels sprout skins

Preparation time: 15 minutes | Dehydration time: 6 hours | Servings: 4

Ingredients:

- 4 cups brussels sprouts, coarsely chopped, tough centers discarded
- 1 cup buttermilk
- 1 tsp. Mustard
- 3 tbsp. Oil
- 1/2 tsp. Salt
- 1 tsp. Onion powder
- 1 tsp. Minced garlic flakes
- 1 tsp. Dried dill
- 1 tsp. Dried parsley
- 1 tsp. Celery salt

Direction:

1. Place sliced brussels sprouts in a bowl. Blend the seasonings in another small bowl.
2. Whisk together buttermilk, mustard and oil. Pour over brussels sprouts.
3. Spray dehydrator tray with nonstick spray and place brussels sprouts on tray. Sprinkle with seasonings. Set the dehydrator to 110 degrees and dehydrate for 8-6 hours.

Nutrition Calories: 16, sodium: 104 mg, dietary fiber: 0.8 g, total fat: 0.2 g, total carbs: 3 g, protein: 1.1 g.

Root vegetable medley

Preparation time: 15 minutes | Dehydration time: 6 hours | Servings: 4

Ingredients:

- 2 medium beets
- 1 sweet potato
- 2 medium parsnips
- 1 medium celery root
- 3 tbsp. Olive oil
- 1 1/2 tsp. Salt
- 1 tsp. Garlic powder
- 1/2 tsp. Oregano
- Pinch of black pepper

Direction:

1. Wash, peel and slice vegetables as thinly as possible, preferably with a mandolin.
2. Place vegetables in a bowl. Mix olive oil with seasonings and pour over vegetables. Toss to coat.
3. Lay vegetables on trays using different trays for different

vegetables. Dehydrate at 105 degrees for at least 8 hours.

Nutrition Calories:: 48, sodium: 737 mg, dietary fiber: 2.1 g, total fat: 0.2 g, total carbs: 11 g, protein: 1.3 g.

Salt & pepper vinegar zucchini chips

Preparation time: 15 minutes | Dehydration time: 6 hours | Servings: 4

Ingredients:

- 2 large green zucchini, cut into 1/8" thick rounds
- 3-4 tsp. Olive oil
- 1 tbsp. + 1 tsp. Apple cider vinegar
- Salt & pepper to taste

Direction:

1. Toss zucchini slices with olive oil until well coated. Add vinegar, salt and pepper and combine.
2. Spread zucchini onto a dehydrator tray.
3. Set the dehydrator to 135 degrees and dehydrate for 10-12 hours. Halfway through, flip each chip over to prevent sticking.

Nutrition Calories: 7, sodium: 338 mg, dietary fiber: 0 g, total fat: 0 g, total carbs: 1.8 g, protein: 0.2 g.

Salt and vinegar cucumber chips

Preparation time: 15 minutes | Dehydration time: 6 hours | Servings: 4

Ingredients:

- 2 large cucumbers, peeled and sliced thins

- 2 tsp. Apple cider vinegar
- 1 tsp. Fresh lemon juice
- 1/2 tsp. Kosher salt
- 1/2 tsp. Sugar

Direction:

1. In a bowl, whisk together vinegar, lemon juice, salt and sugar. Add cucumbers and toss in dressing.
2. Place cucumber slices on dehydrator tray and dehydrate for 4-6 hours at 135 degrees.

Nutrition Calories:: 6, sodium: 0 mg, dietary fiber: 0.6 g, total fat: 0 g, total carbs: 1.2 g, protein: 0.3 g.

Sweet kale chips

Preparation time: 15 minutes | Dehydration time: 6 hours | Servings: 4

Ingredients:

- 1 bunch curly kale, washed, tough stems removed and leaves roughly torn
- 1/2 cup pine nuts
- 1/8-1/4 cup white sugar
- 1/2 tbsp. Cinnamon
- 1/3 cup water
- 1/8 cup apple cider vinegar

Direction:

1. Place pine nuts, sugar and cinnamon in a food processor.
2. Blend water and vinegar and add slowly to food processor.
3. Pour mixture over kale and mix until coated.
4. Place on dehydrating trays for 2-4 hours at 140 degrees.

Nutrition Calories:: 108, sodium: 5 mg, dietary fiber: 1.3 g, total fat:

7.9 g, total carbs: 9.4 g, protein: 1.9 g.

Sweet and savory beet rounds

Preparation time: 15 minutes | Dehydration time: 6 hours | Servings: 4

Ingredients:

- 4 large beets, washed
- 2 tbsp. Olive oil
- 1 tsp. Fresh rosemary, finely chopped
- 1/2 tsp. Sea salt
- 1/4 tsp. Pepper

Direction:

1. Cut tops of beets. Slice beets about 1/8-1/4 inch wide. Use a mandolin if possible.
2. Toss beets, olive oil, rosemary, salt and pepper in a bowl until evenly coated.
3. Set the dehydrator to 145 degrees. Place trays in dehydrator for 10-12 hours.

Nutrition Calories:: 21, sodium: 539 mg, dietary fiber: 1.9 g, total fat: 0.5 g, total carbs: 4.6 g, protein: 0.6 g.

Tex-mex green beans

Preparation time: 15 minutes | Dehydration time: 6 hours | Servings: 4

Ingredients:

- 5 pounds green beans
- 1/3 cup melted coconut oil

- 1 tsp. Chili powder
- 1 tsp. Cumin
- 1/2 tsp. Each paprika, onion powder, garlic powder, salt and pepper

Direction:

1. Blanch green beans in boiling water for several minutes. Dry beans.
2. Melt coconut oil in microwave. Mix oil and seasonings in a bowl.
3. Coast green beans in oil mixture.
4. Place green beans onto dehydrator and dry for 8-6 hours at 125 degrees.

Nutrition Calories:: 12, sodium: 7 mg, dietary fiber: 1.1 g, total fat: 0.2 g, total carbs: 2.4 g, protein: 0.6 g.

Vegan broccoli crisps

Preparation time: 15 minutes | Dehydration time: 6 hours | Servings: 4

Ingredients:

- 2 heads broccoli, washed and cut into bite size florets
- 1/2 cup cashews, soaked for at least 1 hour and drained
- 4 tbsp. Nutritional yeast
- 1 tsp. Curry powder
- 1/2 tsp. Red pepper flakes

Direction:

1. Blend the cashews, nutritional yeast and spices in a food processor. Add water to achieve a smooth texture. Nuts should be fully blended.
2. Pour dressing into a bowl and add broccoli. Coat the florets

evenly.

3. Place florets onto dehydrator sheets and dehydrate at 110 degrees for 18 hours.

Nutrition Calories:: 104, sodium: 8 mg, dietary fiber: 2.3 g, total fat: 6.8 g, total carbs: 8 g, protein: 5.1 g.

Crackers Bread and Chips

Carrot crackers

Preparation time: 20 minutes | Dehydration time: 6 hours | Servings: 10

Ingredients:

- 1 cup almonds, soaked overnight, rinsed, and drained
- 2 cups carrot pulp
- 1 tablespoon ground chia seeds
- 2 tablespoons ground flax seed
- 1 teaspoon italian seasoning
- 1 tablespoon coconut aminos
- 1/2 teaspoon smoked paprika
- 1 tablespoon dried onion
- 1/2 teaspoon red pepper flakes
- 2 cups water

Direction:

1. Add the almonds to a food processor or blender.
2. Pulse until crumbly.
3. Stir in the rest of the ingredients.
4. Pulse until fully combined.
5. Spread a thin layer of the dough in the cosori premium food dehydrator.
6. Dry at 125 degrees f for 2 hours.
7. Score the dough to form the crackers.
8. Dry at 115 degrees for 8 hours.
9. Storage suggestions: store in an airtight food container for up to 5 days.

Tip: soak the almonds overnight the day before processing.

Nutrition Calories:: 122 fat: 7.4 g, carbs: 10.8 g protein: 3.9 g.

Sweet potato chips

Preparation time: 15 minutes | Dehydration time: 4 hours | Servings: 2

Ingredients:

- 2 sweet potatoes, scrubbed and sliced thinly
- Salt to taste
- 2 teaspoons onion powder

Direction:

1. Arrange the sweet potatoes in the cosori premium food dehydrator.
2. Process at 155 degrees f for 2 hours.
3. Flip and dry for another 2 hours.
4. Sprinkle with salt and onion powder.
5. Storage suggestions: store in a sealable plastic bag.

Tip: use homemade onion powder.

Nutrition: calories 195, fat 3, fiber 1, carbs 20, protein 4

☆ ☆ ☆ ☆ ☆

Tomato & flaxseed crackers

Preparation time: 20 minutes | Dehydration time: 8 hours | Servings: 24

Ingredients:

- 1 cup flaxseed
- 8 sun-dried tomatoes
- 1 bell pepper, chopped
- 1tablespoon olive oil
- Salt to taste
- 2 tomatoes, chopped
- 1 onion, chopped
- 1 clove garlic, crushed through garlic press

- 1/4 cup dried oregano leaves, crushed
- Salt and pepper to taste

Direction:

1. Place the flaxseed in a bowl.
2. In another bowl, combine the remaining ingredients.
3. Stir in the flaxseeds.
4. Combine all the ingredients in the food processor.
5. Pulse until fully combined.
6. Spread the mixture in the cosori premium food dehydrator.
7. Process at 110 degrees f for 12 hours.
8. Storage suggestions: store in an airtight jar for up to 9 days.

Tip: soak the flaxseeds in water for 2 hours before processing.

Nutrition: Calories: 178, Fat: 13.3g, Carbs: 10.7g, Protein: 4.4g

Seed crackers

Preparation time: x hours | Dehydration time: x hours | Servings: 10

Ingredients:

- 1/4 cup chia seeds
- 3/4 cup flax seeds
- 1 cup water
- 1/4 cup hemp seeds
- 1/3 cup sunflower seeds
- 2 tablespoons pumpkin seeds
- 1 tablespoon italian seasoning
- Salt and pepper to taste

Direction:

1. Soak the chia seeds and flax seeds in water for 1 hour.
2. Drain.

3. Transfer to a bowl.
4. Stir in the rest of the ingredients.
5. Process at 115 degrees f for 90 minutes.
6. Flip and break into smaller pieces.
7. Dry at 105 degrees f for 8 hours.
8. Storage suggestions: store in an airtight container for up to 7 days.

Tip: serve with hummus.

Nutrition: Calories: 178, Fat: 13.3g, Carbs: 10.7g, Protein: 4.4g

☆ ☆ ☆ ☆ ☆

Apple chips with cinnamon

Preparation time: 15 minutes | Dehydration time: 8 hours | Servings: 4

Ingredients:

- 4 apples, sliced thinly
- 1/4 cup sugar
- 1 tablespoon ground cinnamon

Direction:

1. Mix the cinnamon and sugar.
2. Coat the apple slices with this mixture.
3. Place the apple slices in the cosori premium food dehydrator.
4. Process at 135 degrees f for 12 hours.
5. Storage suggestions: store in an airtight food container.

Tip: use a mandoliner slicer to slice the apples thinly.

Nutrition: calories 195, fat 3, fiber 1, carbs 20, protein 4

☆ ☆ ☆ ☆ ☆

Vegan bread

Preparation time: 30 minutes | Dehydration time: 6 hours | Servings: 4

Ingredients:

- 1 head cauliflower
- 1 teaspoon turmeric
- 2 tablespoons flax seed
- 1/2 cup psyllium hust
- 1/2 cup brewer's yeast
- 4 large zucchini
- Salt and black pepper

Directions:

1. Place cauliflower and zucchini in a food processor and pulse until they form a paste. Add the turmeric, flax seeds, psyllium, yeast, and a pinch of salt and black pepper. Pulse again until all ingredients are thoroughly combined.
2. Place paraflexx screens on the racks of your excalibur food dehydrator. Form the mixture into slices about 1/2-inch-thick, and place on the screens.
3. Set your excalibur to 150f and dehydrate for 6 hours. The bread should not be completely dry. One side should be slightly soft.

Nutrition Calories: 219 fat: 1.9 g, carbs: 61.6 g protein: 10.1 g.

Fluffy dinner rolls

Preparation time: 15 minutes | Dehydration time: 7 hours |Servings: 4

Ingredients:

- 2 cups almond flour

- 1 cup psyllium
- 3 tablespoons ground flax seeds
- 1 tablespoon onion powder
- 2 teaspoons garlic powder
- 1 tablespoon lemon juice
- 1 teaspoon salt
- 1/3 cup water

Directions:

1. In a large bowl, combine the flour, psyllium, flax seeds, onion powder, garlic powder, lemon juice, salt, and water. Mix well until combined.
2. Form the mixture into 6 round rolls.
3. Place paraflexx screens on the racks of your excalibur. Place the rolls on the screens so they are not touching. Dehydrate at 145f for one hour, and then lower the temperature to 110f for the remaining 6 hours. Remove from the screens and serve warm or allow cooling before storing.

Nutrition Calories: 319 fat: 7.1 g,carbs: 95.2 g protein: 3.5 g.

☆ ☆ ☆ ☆ ☆

Herb and almond crackers

Preparation time: 10 minutes | Dehydration time: 12 hours | Servings: 4

Ingredients:

- 2 cups almonds
- 1/2 cup ground flax seeds
- 1/4 cup brewer's yeast
- 3/4 cups water
- 2 tablespoons fresh rosemary, finely chopped
- 1 teaspoon salt
- 1/2 teaspoon black pepper

Directions:

1. In a food processor, combine the almonds, flax seed, yeast, salt, and pepper. Pulse until well combined.
2. Slowly add the water while continuing to pulse until a paste forms.
3. Place paraflexx screens on the racks of your excalibur and spread a thin layer of the paste onto each screen. Set your excalibur to 115f and dehydrate for 12 hours or until the crackers are crispy. Remove from the screens and break into small pieces to serve.

Nutrition Calories: 260 fats: 19.3 g, carbs: 13.3 g protein: 11.6 g.

Carrot crackers

Preparation time: 20 minutes | Dehydration time: 12 hours | Servings: 12

Ingredients:

- 1/2 cup ground flax seeds
- 1 tomato, diced
- Juice from 1 lemon
- 1/2 cup sesame seeds
- 1/2 cup chia seeds
- 3/4 cups water

Directions:

1. In a food processor, combine the carrots, flax seeds, tomato, lemon juice, and water, and pulse until a paste forms. Add the chia seeds and sesame seeds and stir to combine.
2. Place paraflexx screens on the racks of your excalibur food dehydrator. Spread the paste evenly on the screens about 1/4 inch thick.
3. Set your excalibur to 105f and dehydrate for 12 hours.

Remove the crackers from the excalibur and allow cooling completely. The crackers will become crispy as they cool.

Nutrition Calories: 122 fat: 7.4 g, carbs: 10.8 g protein: 3.9 g.

Sweet potato chips

Preparation time: 10 minutes | Dehydration time: 14 hours | Servings: 4

Ingredients:

- 2 large sweet potatoes
- 2 teaspoons coconut oil, melted
- 2 teaspoons salt

Directions:

1. Using a mandolin, slice the potatoes into thin rounds. In a large bowl, combine the potato slices, salt, and coconut oil and toss to coat.
2. Place paraflexx screens on the racks of your excalibur food dehydrator and place the potato slices on the screens in a single layer.
3. Set your excalibur to 125f and dehydrate for 12 to 14 hours or until the potato slices are crisp. Remove from the screens and store in a cool dry place if not using immediately.

Nutrition Calories: 13 fat: 1.5 g carbs: 0.1 g protein: 0 g.

Mexican crackers

Preparation time: 30 minutes | Dehydration time: 6 hours | Servings: 15

Ingredients:

- 1/2 cup chia seeds

- 1 cup golden flaxseeds
- 1/2 cup pumpkin seeds
- 1/2 cup sunflower seeds
- 1 red bell pepper, chopped
- 1/4 onion, chopped
- 1 cup carrot pulp
- 1 1/2 teaspoons chipotle powder
- 1 teaspoon garlic powder
- Salt to taste
- 1/2 teaspoon cayenne pepper

Direction:

1. in a blender process all the seeds until powdery.
2. Stir in the bell pepper and onion.
3. Pulse until smooth.
4. Stir in the rest of the ingredients.
5. Pulse until fully combined.
6. Spread the mixture in the cosori premium food dehydrator.
7. Score the crackers.
8. Dry at 115 degrees f for 6 hours.
9. Storage suggestions: store in a sealed food container for up to 5 days.

Tip: soak the seeds in separate bowls of water for 6 hours before processing.

Nutrition Calories: 122 fat: 7.4 g, carbs: 10.8 g protein: 3.9 g.

Flax crackers

Preparation time: 4 hours and 10 minutes | Dehydration time: 24 hours | Servings: 12 crackers

Ingredients:

- 1 1/2 cups water

- 1 clove garlic, minced
- 3/4 cup golden flax seeds
- 1/4 cup flax seeds
- 3 teaspoons sesame seeds, crushed
- 3 teaspoons poppy seeds, crushed
- 3 teaspoons garlic flakes
- 3 teaspoons onion flakes
- 3 teaspoons salt

Direction:

1. Add the water and garlic in a blender.
2. Blend until smooth.
3. Pour the mixture in a bowl with the flaxseeds.
4. Soak for 4 hours.
5. Spread the gelatin mixture in the cosori premium food dehydrator.
6. Score the crackers with a knife.
7. Combine the remaining ingredients in a bowl.
8. Sprinkle the mixture on top of the crackers.
9. Process at 110 degrees f for 24 hours.
10. Storage suggestions: store in a glass jar with lid for up to 5 days.

Tip: make your own garlic and onion flakes.

Nutrition Calories: 122 fat: 7.4 g, carbs: 10.8 g protein: 3.9 g.

Green crackers

Preparation time: 20 minutes | Dehydration time: 8 hours | Servings: 4

Ingredients:

- 1 cup green juice pulp
- 1/4 cup ground flax seeds

- 1/4 cup chia seeds
- 1/4 cup nutritional yeast
- 2 tablespoons sesame seeds
- 1 tablespoon tamari
- 1/2 teaspoon salt
- 1/4 cup water

Direction:

1. Combine all the ingredients in a bowl.
2. Transfer to a food processor.
3. Pulse until fully combined.
4. Spread a thin layer of the mixture in the cosori premium food dehydrator.
5. Score the crackers.
6. Process at 115 degrees f for 5 hours.
7. Flip the crackers.
8. Dry for another 3 hours.
9. Storage suggestions: store in a sealable plastic bag for up to 7 days.

Tip: the mixture layer should be 1/8 inch thick only.

Nutrition Calories: 122 fat: 7.4 g, carbs: 10.8 g protein: 3.9 g.

Seaweed & tamari crackers

Preparation time: 15 minutes | Dehydration time: 24 hours | Servings: 15

Ingredients:

- 1 cup flax seeds
- 2 nori sheets, broken
- 2 tablespoons tamari
- 1 1/2 cups water

Direction:

1. Mix all the ingredients in a bowl.
2. Spread a layer in the cosori premium food dehydrator.
3. Set it at 110 degrees f.
4. Process for 24 hours.
5. Break into crackers.
6. Storage suggestions: store in a glass jar with lid for up to 5 days.

Tip: soak flaxseeds in water for 1 hour before processing.

Nutrition Calories: 122 fat: 7.4 g, carbs: 10.8 g protein: 3.9 g.

Garlic zucchini chips

Preparation time: 15 minutes | Dehydration time: 4 hours | Servings: 4

Ingredients:

- 3 zucchinis, sliced into thin rounds
- 2 tablespoons olive oil
- 2 tablespoons sesame seeds
- 2 tablespoons dried thyme, crushed
- 2 cloves garlic, grated
- Salt to taste

Direction:

1. Coat the zucchini with olive oil.
2. Sprinkle with the sesame seeds, thyme, garlic and salt.
3. Add these to the cosori premium food dehydrator.
4. Dehydrate at 158 degrees f for 2 hours.
5. Flip and dry for another 2 hours.
6. Storage suggestions: store in a sealable plastic bag.

Tip: before dehydrating, press the zucchini rounds with paper towel to remove excess moisture.

Nutrition: calories 70, fat 4, fiber 4, carbs 30, protein 2

Pear chips

Preparation time: 10 minutes | Dehydration time: 6 hours | Servings: 10

Ingredients:

- 10 pears, cored and sliced thinly

Direction:

1. Arrange the pear slices in the cosori premium food dehydrator.
2. Dehydrate at 145 degrees f for 8 hours.
3. Storage suggestions: store in a sealed food container for up to 7 days.

Tip: make sure the pear slices do not overlap to ensure even crisp.

Nutrition: calories 70, fat 4, fiber 4, carbs 30, protein 2

Banana chips

Preparation time: 15 minutes | Dehydration time: 12 hours | Servings: 4

Ingredients:

- 4 bananas, sliced thinly
- 1 teaspoon lemon juice

Direction:

1. Drizzle the banana slices with lemon juice.
2. Add these to the cosori premium food dehydrator.
3. Process at 135 degrees f for 12 hours.

4. Storage suggestions: store in a vacuum sealed plastic for up to 3 months.

Tip: drizzling bananas with lemon juice prevents browning.

Nutrition: calories 70, fat 4, fiber 4, carbs 30, protein 2

☆ ☆ ☆ ☆ ☆

Sesame & carrot crackers

Preparation time: 45 minutes | Dehydration time: 24 hours | Servings: 15

Ingredients:

- 1 1/2 cups of golden flaxseeds
- 1/4 cup sesame seeds
- 2 cups carrot pulp
- 1 teaspoon of garlic powder
- 1/2 teaspoon of ground coriander
- 3 tablespoons tamari
- 1 cup water

Direction:

1. Grind the flaxseeds in the spice grinder.
2. Add to a bowl along with the remaining ingredients.
3. Mix well.
4. Let sit for 30 minutes.
5. Spread the mixture in the cosori premium food dehydrator.
6. Process at 110 degrees f for 24 hours.
7. Storage suggestions: store in an airtight jar for up to 7 days.

Tip: make your own garlic powder.

Nutrition Calories: 122 fat: 7.4 g, carbs: 10.8 g protein: 3.9 g.

☆ ☆ ☆ ☆ ☆

Peanut butter & banana crackers

Preparation time: 4 hours and 20 minutes | Dehydration time: 6 hours | Servings: 12

Ingredients:

- 3 bananas, sliced
- 1/2 cup peanut butter
- 1/2 teaspoon cinnamon powder
- 1 cup ground peanuts
- 3 cups graham cracker crumbs

Direction:

1. Mash the bananas and peanut butter in a bowl.
2. Stir in the rest of the ingredients.
3. Roll the dough into a large ball.
4. Flatten the ball to form a long rectangle.
5. Wrap the dough with wax paper and refrigerate for 4 hours.
6. Roll out the dough and slice.
7. Add the slices to the cosori premium food dehydrator.
8. Process at 145 degrees f for 6 hours.
9. Storage suggestions: store in a glass jar with lid for up to 5 days.

Tip: do not skip refrigerating the dough before the dehydration process.

Nutrition: Calories: 178, Fat: 13.3g, Carbs: 10.7g, Protein: 4.4g

★ ★ ★ ★ ☆

Side Dishes

Zucchini chips

Preparation time: 15 minutes | Dehydration time: 12 hours | Servings: 8

Ingredients:

- 4 cups zucchini, sliced thinly
- 2 tbsp. Balsamic vinegar
- 2 tbsp. Olive oil
- 2 tsp. Sea salt

Direction:

1. Add olive oil, balsamic vinegar, and sea salt to the large bowl and stir well.
2. Add sliced zucchini to the bowl and toss well.
3. Arrange zucchini slices on dehydrator trays and dehydrate at 135 f/ 58 c for 8-12 hours.
4. Store in air-tight container.

Nutrition Calories: 40 fat: 3.6g protein: 0.7g carbs: 1.9g

Eggplant slices

Preparation time: 10 minutes | Dehydration time: 4 hours | Servings: 4

Ingredients:

- 1 medium eggplant, cut into 1/4 inch thick slices
- 1/4 tsp. Onion powder
- 1/4 tsp. Garlic powder
- 1 1/2 tsp. Paprika

Directions:

1. Add all ingredients into the mixing bowl and toss well.
2. Arrange eggplant slices on dehydrator trays and dehydrate at 145 f/ 63 c for 4 hours or until crispy.

3. Store in air-tight container.

Nutrition Calories: 32 fat: 0.3g protein: 1.3g carbs: 7.4g

☆ ☆ ☆ ☆ ☆

Tasty zucchini chips

Preparation time: 15 minutes | Dehydration time: 8 hours | Servings: 4

Ingredients:

- 2 medium zucchini wash and cut into 1/4 inch slices
- 1/8 tsp. Cayenne pepper
- 1/2 tsp. Garlic powder
- 1 tsp. Olive oil
- 1/8 tsp. Sea salt

Direction:

1. Add all ingredients into the mixing bowl and toss well to coat.
2. Arrange zucchini slices on dehydrator trays and dehydrate at 135 f/ 58 c for 6-8 hours.
3. Store in air-tight container.

Nutrition Calories: 27 fat: 1.4g protein: 1.3g carbs: 3.6g

☆ ☆ ☆ ☆ ☆

Brussels sprout chips

Preparation time: 15 minutes | Dehydration time: 6 hours | Servings: 4

Ingredients:

- 2 lbs. Brussels sprouts, wash, dry, cut the root and separate leaves
- 2 fresh lemon juice
- 1/2 cup water

- 1/4 cup nutritional yeast
- 1 jalapeno pepper halved and remove seeds
- 1 cup cashews
- 2 bell peppers
- 1 tsp. Sea salt

Directions:

1. Add brussels sprouts leaves to the large bowl and set aside.
2. Add bell peppers, water, lemon juice, nutritional yeast, jalapeno, cashews, and salt to the blender and blend until smooth.
3. Pour blended mixture over brussels sprouts leaves and toss until well coated.
4. Arrange brussels sprouts on dehydrator trays and dehydrate at 125 f/ 52 c for 6 hours.
5. Allow to cool completely then store in air-tight container.

Nutrition Calories: 237 fat: 11.7g protein: 12.3g carbs: 27.7g

Bbq jerky strips

Preparation time: 15 minutes | Dehydration time: 6 hours | Servings: 4

Ingredients:

- 2 1/2 pounds lean ground beef
- 2 tsp. Salt
- 1/2 tsp. Garlic powder
- 1/2 tsp. Onion powder
- 1 1/2 tbsp. Brown sugar
- 1/4 cup worcestershire sauce
- 1/2 cup barbecue sauce, slightly diluted with water

Direction:

1. Mix ground beef with dry ingredients until incorporated.

2. Combine liquids and coat beef strips with sauce.
3. Press strips into jerky gun. Squeeze onto dehydrator trays and dry at 145-155 degrees for 6-12 hours.

Nutrition Calories:: 54, sodium: 329 mg, dietary fiber: 0 g, total fat: 1.2 g, total carbs: 4.6 g, protein: 5.8 g.

Bold beef jerky

Preparation time: 15 minutes | Dehydration time: 6 hours | Servings: 4

Ingredients:

- 2 pounds sliced lean meat
- 1/4 cup soy sauce
- 1 tbsp. Worcestershire sauce
- 1 tsp. Hot sauce
- 1/4 tsp. Pepper
- 1/4 tsp. Garlic powder
- 1/4 tsp. Onion powder
- 1/4 tsp. Paprika
- 1 tsp. Liquid smoke

Direction:

1. Cut strips into 1/4 inch thick slices.
2. Mix all ingredients and coat meat strips.
3. Cover and refrigerate overnight.
4. Place meat slices on dehydrator trays and dry at 145-155 degrees for 6-6 hours.

Nutrition Calories:: 51, sodium: 27 mg, dietary fiber: 0 g, total fat: 1.7 g, total carbs: 0 g, protein: 8.3 g.

Orange flavored beef jerky

Preparation time: 15 minutes | Dehydration time: 6 hours | Servings: 4

Ingredients:

- 3 pounds lean beef, trimmed of all fat and sliced into strips 1/8 inches -3/8 inches thick
- 3 oranges, (2 peeled and juiced, and 1 zested)
- 3 tbsp. Soy sauce
- 3 tbsp. Rice vinegar
- 2 tbsp. Sugar
- 3 tbsp. Sesame oil
- 1 1/2 tbsp. Toasted sesame oil
- 1 tsp. Asian chili-garlic paste
- 2 tbsp. Fresh ginger, grated

Direction:

1. Place all the ingredients, except for the beef, into a blender and process until smooth.
2. Pour marinade over meat and mix.
3. Keep marinated meat in refrigerator overnight.
4. Remove from refrigerator and let meat come to room temperature.
5. Lay meat on dehydrator sheets in a single layer.
6. Dehydrate at 145-160 degrees for 6-6 hours.

Nutrition Calories:: 61, sodium: 16 mg, dietary fiber: 0 g, total fat: 1.6 g, total carbs: 4.3 g, protein: 7.3 g.

Pastrami jerky

Ingredients:

- 3 pounds lean beef, such as flank

- 1/2 cup soy sauce
- 1/4 cup brown sugar
- 1/2 cup worcestershire sauce
- 1 tbsp. Lemon juice
- 1/2 tsp. Cayenne pepper
- 2 tbsp. Coarse pepper seeds
- 2 tbsp. Coriander seeds
- 1 tbsp. Mustard seeds

Direction:

1. Cut each slice of beef into 1/4 inch thick strips.
2. Combine all ingredients except seeds. Pour ingredients over sliced meat and refrigerate overnight.
3. Remove from refrigerator and let meat come to room temperature.
4. Lay meat on dehydrator sheets and sprinkle with seeds.
5. Dehydrate at 145-155 degrees for 6-6 hours.

Nutrition Calories:: 56, sodium: 50 mg, dietary fiber: 0 g, total fat: 1.4 g, total carbs: 4.2 g, protein: 6.1 g.

Salmon jerky

Preparation time: 15 minutes | Dehydration time: 6 hours | Servings: 4

Ingredients:

- 1 1/2 pounds salmon, bones removed
- 1/4 cup soy sauce
- 1/4 cup teriyaki sauce
- 1 tbsp. Dijon mustard
- 1 tbsp. Maple syrup
- 1 freshly squeezed lime
- 1/2 tsp. Black pepper

Directions:

1. Freeze salmon for 45 minutes to 1 hour prior to slicing.
2. Place remaining ingredients in a bowl and whisk together.
3. Slice salmon into thin strips and add them to the liquid. Marinate for 3 hours.
4. Remove salmon strips, pat dry and place on dehydrator sheets.
5. Dehydrate for 10-12 hours at 155 degrees.

Nutrition Calories:: 36, sodium: 166 mg, dietary fiber: 0 g, total fat: 1.4 g, total carbs: 1.3 g, protein: 4.7 g.

"Smoked" turkey

Preparation time: 15 minutes | Dehydration time: 6 hours | Servings: 4

Ingredients:

- 1 pound, skinless, boneless turkey
- 1/4 cup brown sugar
- 3/4 cup soy sauce
- 2 tbsp. Liquid smoke
- 1 tbsp. Smoked paprika
- 1/2 tbsp. Paprika

Direction:

1. Slice turkey into 1/4 inch thick strips.
2. Combine all ingredients and pour over turkey strips. Cover turkey and refrigerate 4-6 hours.
3. Place turkey slices on dehydrator trays and dry at 155 degrees for 12-16 hours. Rotate trays occasionally to ensure consistent dehydration.

Nutrition Calories:: 72, sodium: 14 mg, dietary fiber: 1.2 g, total fat: 1.5 g, total carbs: 10 g, protein: 5.6 g.

☆ ☆ ☆ ☆ ☆

Smokey mexican jerky

Preparation time: 15 minutes | Dehydration time: 6 hours | Servings: 4

Ingredients:

- 2 pounds beef top round or bottom round, fat trimmed, sliced into 1/4 inch thick slices
- 1/2 cup soy sauce
- 1 cup fresh lime juice
- 1-2 canned chipotle peppers in adobo sauce
- 1 tsp. Chili powder
- 1 cup mexican beer

Direction:

1. Place all the ingredients, except for the beef, into a blender and process until smooth.
2. Pour marinade over meat and refrigerate for 6-8 hours.
3. Remove from refrigerator and place meat on dehydrator sheets in a single layer.
4. Dehydrate at 145-160 degrees for 6-6 hours.

Nutrition Calories:: 59, sodium: 24 mg, dietary fiber: 0.6 g, total fat: 1.7 g, total carbs: 2.7 g, protein: 8.2 g.

Spiced "hamburger" jerky

Preparation time: 15 minutes | Dehydration time: 6 hours | Servings: 4

Ingredients:

- 2 1/2 pounds lean ground beef
- 1 tsp. Adobo seasoning

- 2 tsp. Salt
- 1/2 tsp. Garlic powder
- 1/2 tsp. Onion powder
- 1 tbsp. Meat tenderizer
- 1/2 tsp. Cayenne pepper
- 1/4 cup tomato sauce
- 1 1/2 tbsp. Brown sugar
- 1/4 cup worcestershire sauce
- 1/4 cup liquid smoke

Direction:

1. Mix ground beef with dry ingredients until seasonings are well distributed.
2. Combine liquids and coat beef strips with sauce.
3. Press strips into jerky gun. Squeeze onto dehydrator trays and dry at 145-155 degrees for 6-12 hours.

Nutrition Calories:: 52, sodium: 319 mg, dietary fiber: 0 g, total fat: 1.3 g, total carbs: 3.5 g, protein: 6.2 g.

Spiced turkey jerky

Preparation time: 15 minutes | Dehydration time: 6 hours | Servings: 4

Ingredients:

- 2 pounds skinless, boneless turkey
- 3/4 cup soy sauce
- 3 tbsp. Brown sugar
- 2 tsp. Chopped garlic
- 2 tsp. Red chili flakes

Direction:

1. Freeze turkey prior to slicing. Cut into 1/4 inch thick strips.

2. Combine all ingredients and dip turkey strips into mixture.
3. Cover turkey strips and refrigerate overnight.
4. Place turkey slices on dehydrator trays and dry at 155 degrees for 8-6 hours.

Nutrition Calories:: 62, sodium: 17 mg, dietary fiber: 0 g, total fat: 1.4 g, total carbs: 5.1 g, protein: 6.9 g.

Spicy harissa flavored jerky

Preparation time: 15 minutes | Dehydration time: 6 hours | Servings: 4

Ingredients:

- 3 pounds lean beef, such as bottom round or eye of round
- 2 tbsp. Salt
- 1 tbsp. Brown sugar
- 1 tbsp. Chili powder
- 1 tbsp. Smoked paprika
- 1 tbsp. Cumin
- 1 tbsp. Coriander
- 1 tbsp. Garlic powder
- 1 tbsp. Onion powder
- 1/4 tsp. Cayenne pepper

Direction:

1. Cut each slice of beef into 1/4 inch thick strips.
2. Combine ingredients and pour into ziplock bag. Add the meat strips and and refrigerate overnight.
3. Remove from refrigerator and let meat come to room temperature.
4. Lay meat on dehydrator sheets and dehydrate at 145-155 degrees for 6-6 hours.

Nutrition Calories:: 56, sodium: 692 mg, dietary fiber: 0.9 g, total fat: 1.8 g, total carbs: 3.5 g, protein: 6.9 g.

Sweet and spicy venison or beef jerky

Preparation time: 15 minutes | Dehydration time: 6 hours | Servings: 4

Ingredients:

- 2 pounds venison or beef
- 1/2 cup brown sugar
- 1/4 cup pineapple juice
- 1 tbsp. Black pepper
- 1 tbsp. Lemon juice
- 1 tbsp. Minced garlic
- 1 tbsp. Paprika
- 1/4 cup worcestershire sauce
- 1/2 cup soy sauce
- 1 tsp. Sriracha sauce

Direction:

1. Cut pre-frozen venison or beef into 1/4 inch thick slices.
2. Mix all ingredients and coat strips in the sauce.
3. Cover and refrigerate overnight.
4. Place beef or venison slices on dehydrator trays and dry at 145-155 degrees about 6-6 hours.

Nutrition Calories:: 53, sodium: 22 mg, dietary fiber: 1.1 g, total fat: 0.4 g, total carbs: 9.5 g, protein: 3.5 g.

Teriyaki jerky

Preparation time: 15 minutes | Dehydration time: 6 hours | Servings: 4

Ingredients:
- 2 1/2 pounds sliced lean beef
- 1 cup teriyaki sauce
- 1 cup worcestershire sauce
- 1/2 cup soy sauce
- 2 tsp. Onion powder
- 2 tsp. Garlic powder
- 1 tsp. Paprika
- 1 tsp. Ground ginger
- 1 tbsp. Red pepper flakes
- 3 tbsp. Honey
- 1 tsp. Lemon juice

Direction:
1. Cut strips into 1/4 inch thick slices.
2. Mix ingredients together and marinate meat in sauce mixture.
3. Cover and refrigerate overnight.
4. Place meat slices on dehydrator trays and dry at 145-155 degrees for 6-6 hours.

Nutrition Calories:: 48, sodium: 276 mg, dietary fiber: 0 g, total fat: 1 g, total carbs: 5 g, protein: 4.7 g.

Thai sweet chili jerky

Preparation time: 15 minutes | Dehydration time: 6 hours | Servings: 4

Ingredients:
- 2 pounds beef top or bottom round, trimmed, cut into 1/4 inch slices

- 3 tbsp. Soy sauce
- 1 tbsp. Worcestershire sauce
- 1 tbsp. Teriyaki sauce
- 1/2 cup water
- 1 cup sweet chili sauce
- 1 tsp. Ground ginger

Direction:

1. Combine the marinade ingredients in a large bowl. Place meat in a ziplock bag and pour marinade over meat.
2. Marinate meat in refrigerator overnight.
3. Place meat on dehydrator sheets in a single layer.
4. Dehydrate at 155 degrees for 6-8 hours.

Nutrition Calories:: 59, sodium: 131 mg, dietary fiber: 0.6 g, total fat: 1.1 g, total carbs: 5 g, protein: 5.6 g.

Boozy jerky

Preparation time: 15 minutes | Dehydration time: 6 hours | Servings: 4

Ingredients:

- 2 pounds lean steak, trimmed and frozen up to 2 hours prior to slicing
- 16 ounces dark belgian beer
- 2 tbsp. Teriyaki sauce
- 1/4 cup soy sauce
- 2 tbsp. Dark brown sugar
- 1/2 tsp. Seasoned salt
- 2 cloves of garlic, minced
- 1/2 tsp. Cayenne pepper

Direction:

1. Mix the marinade ingredients in a large bowl. Place meat in a ziplock bag and pour marinade over meat.
2. Keep meat in refrigerator overnight.
3. Remove from refrigerator and let meat come to room temperature.
4. Lay meat on dehydrator sheets in a single layer.
5. Dehydrate at 160 degrees for 6-8 hours.

Nutrition Calories:: 60, sodium: 76 mg, dietary fiber: 0 g, total fat: 1.6 g, total carbs: 3.5 g, protein: 7.6 g.

Kale chips

Preparation time: 10 minutes | Dehydration time: 4 hours | Servings: 4

Ingredients:

- 2 kale heads
- 1 tsp. Garlic powder
- 1 tsp. Sea salt
- 1 tbsp. Fresh lemon juice
- 3 tbsp. Nutritional yeast
- 2 tbsp. Olive oil

Directions:

1. Wash kale and cut into bits.
2. Add remaining ingredients into the bowl and mix well.
3. Add kale bits to the bowl and mix until well coated.
4. Arrange kale bits on dehydrator trays and dehydrate at 145 f/ 63 c for 3-4 hours or until crispy.

Nutrition Calories: 111 fat: 7.5g protein: 4.9g carbs: 8.5g

Dried bell peppers

Preparation time: 10 minutes | Dehydration time: 24 hours | Servings: 4

Ingredients:

- 4 bell peppers cut in half and de-seed

Directions:

1. Cut bell peppers in strips then cut each strip in ½ inch pieces.
2. Arrange bell peppers strips on dehydrator racks and dehydrate at 135 f/ 58 c for 12-24 hours or until crisp.
3. Store in air-tight container.

Nutrition Calories: 38 fat: 0.3g protein: 1.2g carbs: 9g

☆ ☆ ☆ ☆ ☆

Avocado chips

Preparation time: 15 minutes | Dehydration time: 6 hours | Servings: 4

Ingredients:

- 4 avocados, halved and pitted
- 1/4 tsp. Sea salt
- 1/4 tsp. Cayenne pepper
- 1/4 cup fresh cilantro, chopped
- 1/2 lemon juice

Directions:

1. Cut avocado into the slices.
2. Drizzle lemon juice over avocado slices.
3. Arrange avocado slices on dehydrator trays and sprinkle with cayenne pepper, salt and cilantro dehydrate at 160 f/ 71 c for 6 hours.

Nutrition Calories: 62 fat: 5.1g protein: 1.1g carbs: 3.2g

☆ ☆ ☆ ☆ ☆

Sweet potato chips

Preparation time: 10 minutes | Dehydration time: 12 hours | Servings:

2 **Ingredients:**

- 2 sweet potatoes peel and sliced thinly
- 1/8 tsp. Ground cinnamon
- 1 tsp. Coconut oil, melted
- Seal salt

Directions:

1. Add sweet potato slices in a bowl. Add cinnamon, coconut oil, and salt and toss well.
2. Arrange sweet potato slices on dehydrator trays and dehydrate at 125 f/ 52 c for 12 hours.
3. Store in air-tight container.

Nutrition Calories: 132 fat: 2.3g protein: 2.1g carbs: 26.3g

☆ ☆ ☆ ☆ ☆

Healthy squash chips

Preparation time: 10 minutes | Dehydration time: 12 hours | Servings: 8

Ingredients:

- 1 yellow squash, cut into 1/8 inch thick slices
- 2 tbsp. Apple cider vinegar
- 2 tsp. Olive oil Salt

Directions:

1. Add all ingredients into the bowl and toss well.
2. Arrange squash slices on dehydrator trays and dehydrate at 115 f/ 46 c for 12 hours or until crispy.

3   Store in air-tight container.

Nutrition Calories: 15 fat: 1.2g protein: 0.3g carbs: 0.9g

Broccoli chips

Preparation time: 15 minutes | Dehydration time: 12 hours | Servings: 4

Ingredients:

- 1 lb. Broccoli, cut into florets
- 1 tsp. Onion powder
- 1 garlic clove
- 1/2 cup vegetable broth
- 1/4 cup hemp seeds
- 2 tbsp. Nutritional yeast

Directions:

1   Add broccoli florets in a large mixing bowl and set aside.
2   Add remaining ingredients into the blender and blend until smooth.
3   Pour blended mixture over broccoli florets and toss well.
4   Arrange broccoli florets on dehydrator trays and dehydrate at 115 f/ 46 c for 10-12 hours.

Nutrition Calories: 106 fat: 4.3g protein: 8.7g carbs: 11.2g

Asian jerky

Preparation time: 15 minutes | Dehydration time: 6 hours | Servings: 4

Ingredients:

- 1 pound sliced lean beef

- 4 tbsp. Soy sauce
- 4 tbsp. Worcestershire sauce
- 1 tsp. Ground ginger
- 1/2 tsp. Pepper
- 3 cloves garlic
- 1 tsp. Toasted sesame oil
- 1 tsp. Honey

Direction:

1   Cut strips into 1/4 inch thick slices.
2   Blend ingredients and coat meat strips in sauce.
3   Cover and refrigerate overnight.
4   Place meat slices on dehydrator trays and dry at 145-155 degrees for 6-6 hours.

Nutrition Calories: 129 Fat 3.6 g Carbohydrates 23 g Protein 2.3 g

Garlicky beef jerky

Preparation time: 15 minutes | Dehydration time: 6 hours | Servings: 4

Ingredients:

- 2 pounds thinly sliced beef
- 1 can of coke
- 7 cloves crushed garlic
- 1/2 cup soy sauce
- 1 tbsp. Worcestershire sauce
- 2 tbsp. Ketchup
- 2 tsp. Red hot sauce
- 1 tsp. Fresh lime juice

Direction:

1   Combine the marinade ingredients in a large bowl. Place meat

in a ziplock bag and pour marinade over meat.

2   Marinate meat in refrigerator for 4-8 hours.

3   Lay meat on dehydrator sheets in a single layer.

4   Dehydrate at 155 degrees for 6-8 hours.

Nutrition Calories:: 52, sodium: 60 mg, dietary fiber: 0 g, total fat: 1.6 g, total carbs: 1.1 g, protein: 7.7 g.

Marinated jerky

Preparation time: 15 minutes | Dehydration time: 6 hours | Servings: 4

Ingredients:

- 2 pounds sliced lean meat
- 1/2 gallon water
- 1/4 cup plus
- 1 tbsp. Salt
- 1/4 cup sugar
- 2 tbsp. Liquid smoke
- 1/2 tsp. Black pepper
- 1/2 tsp. Smoked paprika

Direction:

1   Cut strips into 1/4 inch thick slices. Prepare the brine by mixing all the ingredients.

2   Soak meat strips in the brine overnight.

3   Pour off brine. Rinse and pat meat dry.

4   Place meat slices on dehydrator trays and dry at 145-155 degrees for 6-6 hours.

Nutrition Calories:: 54, sodium: 1,842 mg, dietary fiber: 0 g, total fat: 1.2 g, total carbs: 5 g, protein: 5.8 g.

Meat

Pork jerky in chipotle sauce

Preparation time: 12 hours and 10 minutes | Dehydration time: 6 hours

Servings: 2

Ingredients:

- 1 tablespoon tomato paste
- 7 oz. Chipotle adobo sauce
- 1 teaspoon salt
- 1 teaspoon sugar
- 1 teaspoon garlic powder
- 1 lb. Pork tenderloin, sliced

Direction:

1. Mix the tomato paste, chipotle adobo sauce, salt, sugar and garlic powder in a bowl.
2. Transfer to a sealable plastic bag along with the pork tenderloin slices.
3. Seal and refrigerate for 12 hours.
4. Drain the marinade.
5. Add the pork slices to the cosori premium food dehydrator.
6. Process at 158 degrees f for 6 hours.
7. Storage suggestions: place in a glass jar with lid. Store in a cool dry place, away from sunlight.

Tip: pork tenderloin should be sliced at least 5 mm thick.

Nutrition Calories: 54 Fat 0.3 g Carbohydrates 11.3 g Protein 2.5 g

Paprika pork jerky

Preparation time: 12 hours and 10 minutes | Dehydration time: 6 hours

Servings: 2

Ingredients:

- 1 lb. Pork tenderloin, sliced
- 1/2 cup ketchup
- 1 teaspoon onion powder
- 1 teaspoon garlic powder
- 1 teaspoon smoked paprika
- 1 teaspoon ground mustard
- 1 teaspoon chili powder
- Salt and pepper to taste

Direction:

1. Add the ketchup to a bowl.
2. Stir in the onion powder, garlic powder, paprika, mustard, chili powder, salt and pepper.
3. Mix well.
4. Transfer the mixture to a sealable plastic bag.
5. Add the pork to the plastic bag.
6. Seal and refrigerate for 12 hours.
7. Remove the pork from the marinade.
8. Add to the cosori premium food dehydrator.
9. Dry at 158 degrees f for 6 hours.
10. Storage suggestions: store the pork jerky in a glass jar with lid. Store in a cool dry place for up to 2 weeks.

Tip: you can also use garlic salt in place of garlic powder and salt.

Nutrition Calories: 382 Fat 1.2 g Carbs 67.1 g Protein 26.1 g

☆ ☆ ☆ ☆ ☆

Beef bulgogi jerky

Preparation time: 12 hours and 10 minutes | Dehydration time: 6 hours

Servings: 4

Ingredients:

- 2 lb. Beef round, sliced
- 4 tablespoons brown sugar
- 4 tablespoons soy sauce
- 1 tablespoon garlic powder
- 1 tablespoon sesame oil
- Salt to taste

Direction:

1. Place the beef inside a sealable plastic bag.
2. In a bowl, mix the remaining ingredients.
3. Add the mixture to the plastic bag.
4. Place the beef in the refrigerator for 12 hours.
5. Drain the marinade.
6. Add the beef to the cosori premium food dehydrator.
7. Set at 165 degrees f.
8. Process for 6 hours.
9. Storage suggestions: place in a glass jar with lid and store in a cool, dry place.

Tip: slice the beef across the grain. Each slice should be at least 5 mm thick.

Nutrition Calories: 382 Fat 1.2 g Carbs 67.1 g Protein 26.1 g

☆ ☆ ☆ ☆ ☆

Mustard beef jerky with balsamic vinegar

Preparation time: 12 hours and 10 minutes | Dehydration time: 6 hours

Servings: 4

Ingredients:

- 2 lb. Beef round, sliced
- 2 tablespoons olive oil
- 1 tablespoon dijon mustard
- 1 cup balsamic vinegar
- 2 garlic cloves, crushed
- 1 teaspoon salt

Direction:

1   Add the beef to a sealable plastic bag.
2   Combine the rest of the ingredients in a bowl.
3   Mix well.
4   Pour the mixture into the plastic bag.
5   Place in the refrigerator for 12 hours.
6   Drain the marinade.
7   Add the beef slices to the cosori premium food dehydrator.
8   Set the dehydrator to 165 degrees f.
9   Dry for 6 hours.
10 Storage suggestions: keep the beef jerky slices in a glass container with lid. Store in an area away from sunlight.

Tip: you can dehydrate longer for up to 8 hours.

Nutrition Calories: 372 Fat 27.5 g Carbohydrates 9.6 g Protein 24 g

Buffalo jerky

Preparation time: 15 hours and 10 minutes | Dehydration time: 6 hours

Servings: 4

Ingredients:

- 2 lb. Beef round, sliced
- 1 teaspoon salt
- 1 cup buffalo sauce

Direction:

1. Season the beef slices with the salt.
2. Add the buffalo sauce to a bowl.
3. Stir in the seasoned beef.
4. Cover the bowl.
5. Refrigerate for 15 hours.
6. Drain the marinade.
7. Add the beef slices to the cosori premium food dehydrator.
8. Process at 165 degrees f for 6 hours.
9. Storage suggestions: place the beef jerky in a sealable glass container. Store for up to 2 weeks.

Tip: you can also add hot sauce to the marinade for extra zing.

Nutrition Calories: 372 Fat 27.5 g Carbohydrates 9.6 g Protein 24 g

Barbecue beef jerky

Preparation time: 12 hours and 10 minutes | Dehydration time: 6 hours

Servings: 4

Ingredients:

- 2 lb. Beef round, sliced
- Salt and pepper to taste

- 2 teaspoons dried oregano
- 2 teaspoons ground cumin
- 1 teaspoon onion powder
- 1 teaspoon ground coriander
- 4 cloves garlic, grated
- 1/2 cup olive oil
- 1/2 cup lime juice
- 1 teaspoon red pepper flakes

Direction:

1. Add the beef slices to a sealable plastic bag.
2. In a bowl, mix the salt, pepper, herbs, spices, garlic, olive oil, lime juice and red pepper flakes.
3. Pour mixture into the plastic bag.
4. Turn to coat beef slices evenly with the mixture.
5. Seal and marinate for 12 hours.
6. Drain the marinade.
7. Place the beef slices to the cosori food dehydrator dehydrator.
8. Set it to 165 degrees f and process for 6 hours.
9. Storage suggestions: keep the beef jerky in a vacuum sealed plastic bag.

Tip: you can also use lemon juice instead of lime juice.

Nutrition Calories: 372 Fat 27.5 g Carbohydrates 9.6 g Protein 24 g

Sweet & sour pork

Preparation time: 12 hours and 10 minutes | Dehydration time: 6 hours

Servings: 4

Ingredients:

- 1 lb. Pork tenderloin, sliced

- 2 tablespoons fish sauce
- 1/4 cup lime juice
- 1/4 cup brown sugar
- 1shallot, grated
- 2 garlic cloves, grated
- Salt and pepper to taste

Direction:

1   Combine all the ingredients in a bowl.
2   Mix well.
3   Transfer to a sealable plastic bag.
4   Chill in the refrigerator for 12 hours.
5   Remove from the marinade.
6   Transfer the pork slices to the cosori premium food dehydrator.
7   Process at 158 degrees f for 6 hours.
8   Storage suggestions: store in a glass jar with lid, away from direct sunlight.

Tip: see to it that the slices are at least 5 mm thick.

Nutrition Calories: 372 Fat 27.5 g Carbohydrates 9.6 g Protein 24 g

Lamb jerky

Preparation time: 13 hours | Dehydration time: 6 hours | Servings: 4

Ingredients:

- 3 lb. Leg of lamb, sliced
- 1/4 cup soy sauce
- 3 tablespoons worcestershire sauce
- 1 tablespoon oregano
- 1 teaspoon garlic powder
- 1 1/2 teaspoons onion powder

- Pepper to taste

Direction:

1. Add the lamb slices to a sealable plastic bag.
2. Combine the remaining ingredients in a bowl.
3. Mix well.
4. Pour the mixture into a sealable plastic bag.
5. Marinate in the refrigerator for 13 hours.
6. Place the lamb slices to the cosori premium food dehydrator.
7. Process at 145 degrees f for 6 hours.
8. Storage suggestions: store the lamb jerky in a glass jar with lid for up to 2 weeks.

Tip: freeze the lamb for 1 hour first so it will be easier to slice into strips.

Nutrition Calories: 183 Fat 5 g Carbs 28 g Protein 7.3 g

Beef jerky

Preparation time: 10 minutes | Dehydration time: 6 hours | Servings: 4

Ingredients:

- 2 lb. Beef eye of round
- 1/2 cup soy sauce
- 1/2 cup worcestershire sauce
- 1 teaspoon salt
- 1 tablespoon honey

Direction:

1. Slice the beef eye of round across the grain.
2. Add the soy sauce, worcestershire sauce, salt and honey in a sealable plastic bag.
3. Add the beef to the plastic bag.

4   Turn to coat.

5   Place inside the refrigerator for 12 hours.

6   Drain the marinade.

7   Add the beef to the cosori premium food dehydrator.

8   Process at 165 degrees f for 6 hours.

9   Storage tips: store in a cool dry place. Store in a glass jar with lid for up to 2 weeks.

Tip: slices should be about 5 mm thick.

Nutrition Calories:: 59, sodium: 131 mg, dietary fiber: 0.6 g, total fat: 1.1 g, total carbs: 5 g, protein: 5.6 g.

Candied bacon

Preparation time: 12 hours and 10 minutes | Dehydration time: 6 hours

Servings: 4

Ingredients:

- 10 slices bacon
- 3 tablespoons brown sugar
- 3 tablespoons soy sauce
- 2 teaspoons mirin
- 2 teaspoons sesame oil
- 2 tablespoons chili garlic sauce

Direction:

1   Slice each bacon strip into 3 portions.

2   Add the rest of the ingredients in a bowl.

3   Mix well.

4   Add the bacon slices in the mixture.

5   Cover and refrigerate for 12 hours.

6   Add the bacon to the cosori premium food dehydrator.

7   Dehydrate at 165 degrees f for 6 hours.

8   Storage tips: store candied bacon in a glass jar with lid for up to 2 weeks.

Tip: add chili powder to the marinade if you want your candied bacon extra spicy.

Nutrition Calories:: 59, sodium: 131 mg, dietary fiber: 0.6 g, total fat: 1.1 g, total carbs: 5 g, protein: 5.6 g.

Beef teriyaki jerky

Preparation time: 12 hours and 10 minutes | Dehydration time: 6 hours

Servings: 4

Ingredients:

- 2 lb. Beef round, sliced
- 1/4 cup brown sugar
- 1/2 cup soy sauce
- 1/4 cup pineapple juice
- 1 clove garlic, crushed
- 1/4 teaspoon ginger, grated

Direction:

1   Add all the ingredients in a bowl.
2   Mix well.
3   Transfer to a sealable plastic bag.
4   Add the beef to the plastic bag.
5   Marinate in the refrigerator for 12 hours.
6   Discard the marinade before dehydrating.
7   Add to the cosori premium food dehydrator.
8   Process at 165 degrees f for 6 hours.
9   Storage suggestions: keep in a glass jar with lid or vacuum sealed bag.

Tip: beef should be sliced at least 5 mm thick.

Nutrition Calories: 129 Fat 3.6 g Carbohydrates 23 g Protein 2.3 g

☆ ☆ ☆ ☆ ☆

Vietnamese beef jerky

Preparation time: 12 hours and 10 minutes | Dehydration time: 6 hours

Servings: 4

Ingredients:

- 2 lb. Beef round
- 3 tablespoons fish sauce
- 1 tablespoon soy sauce
- 2 tablespoons lime juice
- 1/4 cup brown sugar

Direction:

1. Combine all the ingredients in a bowl.
2. Transfer to a sealable plastic bag.
3. Turn to coat the beef strips evenly with the marinade.
4. Place in the refrigerator for 12 hours.
5. Drain the marinade.
6. Add the beef to the cosori premium food dehydrator.
7. Process at 165 degrees f for 6 hours.
8. Storage suggestions: store the jerky in a glass jar with lid for up to 1 week.

Tip: slice the beef across the grain. Make sure beef is at least 5 mm thick.

Nutrition Calories: 129 Fat 3.6 g Carbohydrates 23 g Protein 2.3 g

☆ ☆ ☆ ☆ ☆

Smoked herbed bacon jerky

Preparation time: 10 minutes | Dehydration time: 6 hours | Servings: 4

Ingredients:

- 10 slices smoked bacon
- 1 teaspoon ground fennel seeds
- 1/8 teaspoon onion powder
- 1/8 teaspoon garlic powder
- 1/4 teaspoon dried sage
- 1/4 teaspoon dried thyme
- 1 teaspoon brown sugar
- 1/4 teaspoon red pepper flakes
- 1/8 teaspoon black pepper

Direction:

1. Slice the bacon into 3 portions.
2. In a bowl, mix the rest of the ingredients.
3. Sprinkle both sides of the bacon with the seasoning mixture.
4. Add the bacon slices to the cosori premium food dehydrator.
5. Dehydrate at 165 degrees f for 6 hours.
6. Storage suggestions: store the bacon jerky in a glass jar with lid for up to 1 week.

Tip: you can add more red pepper flakes if you want the jerky to be spicier.

Nutrition Calories: 54 Fat 0.3 g Carbohydrates 11.3 g Protein 2.5 g

☆ ☆ ☆ ☆ ☆

Lemon fish jerky

Preparation time: 4 hours and 10 minutes | Dehydration time: 8 hours

Servings: 2

Ingredients:

- 1 lb. Cod fillet, sliced
- 1 tablespoon lemon juice
- 1 teaspoon lemon zest
- 2 tablespoons olive oil
- 1 teaspoon dill
- 1 clove garlic, grated Salt to taste

Direction:

1. Combine the fish slices and the rest of the ingredients in a sealable plastic bag.
2. Turn to coat the fish evenly with the marinade.
3. Place the plastic bag inside the refrigerator for 4 hours.
4. Drain the marinade.
5. Add the fish slices to the cosori premium food dehydrator.
6. Process at 145 degrees f for 8 hours.
7. Storage suggestions: store the fish jerky in a glass jar with lid or vacuum sealed bag for up to 2 weeks.

Tip: you can also use salmon for this recipe.

Nutrition Calories: 183 Fat 5 g Carbs 28 g Protein 7.3 g

☆ ☆ ☆ ☆ ☆

Salmon jerky

Preparation time: 4 hours and 10 minutes | Dehydration time: 8 hours

Servings: 2

Ingredients:

- 1 1/4 lb. Salmon, sliced
- 1/2 cup soy sauce
- 1 tablespoon molasses
- 1 tablespoon lemon juice Pepper to taste

Direction:

1. Place the salmon slices in a sealable plastic bag.
2. Combine the rest of the ingredients in a bowl.
3. Add the mixture to the plastic bag.
4. Marinate inside the refrigerator for 4 hours.
5. Drain the marinade.
6. Add the salmon slices to the cosori premium food dehydrator
7. Process at 145 degrees f for 8 hours.
8. Storage suggestions: place the fish jerky in a food container with lid. Store for up to 2 weeks.

Tip: use freshly squeezed lemon juice. Salmon slices should be 1/4 inch thick.

Nutrition Calories: 183 Fat 5 g Carbs 28 g Protein 7.3 g

Fish teriyaki jerky

Preparation time: 4 hours and 10 minutes | Dehydration time: 8 hours

Servings: 2

Ingredients:

- 1 lb. Salmon, sliced

- 1/4 teaspoon ginger, grated
- 1/4 cup sugar
- 1/2 cup soy sauce
- 1/4 cup orange juice
- 1 clove garlic, minced

Direction:

1. Combine all the ingredients in a bowl.
2. Mix well.
3. Transfer to a sealable plastic bag.
4. Seal and refrigerate for 4 hours.
5. Drain the marinade.
6. Add the salmon to the cosori premium food dehydrator.
7. Process at 145 degrees f for 8 hours.
8. Storage suggestions: store the salmon jerky in a glass jar with lid.

Tip: you can process longer in the dehydrator if you want the fish slices crispier and dryer.

Nutrition Calories: 389 Fat 6.4 g Carbs 22.9 g Protein 49.3 g

Cajun fish jerky

Preparation time: 4 hours and 10 minutes | Dehydration time: 8 hours

Servings: 2

Ingredients:

- 1 teaspoon garlic powder
- 1 teaspoon paprika
- 1 teaspoon onion powder
- 1/4 teaspoon cayenne pepper
- 1 tablespoon lemon juice

- Salt and pepper to taste
- 1 lb. Cod fillet, sliced

Direction:

1. Mix the spices, lemon juice, salt and pepper in a bowl.
2. Season the fish with this mixture.
3. Transfer the seasoned fish and marinade in a sealable plastic bag.
4. Marinate in the refrigerator for 4 hours.
5. Drain the marinade.
6. Arrange the salmon slices on the cosori premium food dehydrator.
7. Process at 145 degrees f for 8 hours.
8. Storage suggestions: store in a vacuum sealed plastic bag or glass jar with lid.

Tip: you can use other white fish fillet for this recipe.

Nutrition Calories: 389 Fat 6.4 g Carbs 22.9 g Protein 49.3 g

Venison jerky

Preparation time: 1 day and 30 minutes | Dehydration time: 4 hours

Servings: 2

Ingredients:

- 1 lb. Venison roast, silver skin trimmed and sliced thinly
- 4 tablespoons coconut amino
- 1/4 teaspoon onion powder
- 1/4 teaspoon garlic powder
- 1/4 teaspoon red pepper flakes
- 1 tablespoon honey
- 4 tablespoons worcestershire sauce

- Salt and pepper to taste

Direction:

1. Place the venison roast slices in a bowl.
2. In another bowl, combine the rest of the ingredients.
3. Pour this mixture into the first bowl.
4. Stir to coat meat evenly with the mixture.
5. Cover the bowl.
6. Chill in the refrigerator for 1 day, stirring every 3 or 4 hours.
7. Drain the marinade.
8. Place the venison slices in the cosori premium food dehydrator.
9. Process at 160 degrees f for 4 hours.
10. Storage suggestions: store in vacuum sealed bags for up to 3 months or in ziplock bags for up to 2 weeks.

Tip: freeze the venison meat for 1 hour before slicing.

Nutrition Calories: 389 Fat 6.4 g Carbs 22.9 g Protein 49.3 g

Hickory smoked jerky

Preparation time: 12 hours and 10 minutes | Dehydration time: 4 hours

Servings: 4

Ingredients:

- 1 lb. Beef round, sliced
- 1/2 cup hickory smoked marinade
- 1/4 cup barbecue sauce
- 2 tablespoons brown sugar
- 1 teaspoon onion powder
- Pinch cayenne pepper
- Salt and pepper to taste

Direction:

1. Place the beef slices in a sealable plastic bag.
2. In a bowl, combine the marinade, barbecue sauce, sugar, onion powder, cayenne, salt and pepper.
3. Pour the mixture into the bag.
4. Seal and marinate in the refrigerator for 12 hours.
5. Discard the marinade and add the beef to the cosori premium food dehydrator.
6. Process at 180 degrees f for 4 hours, flipping halfway through.
7. Storage suggestions: store in a glass jar with lid for up to 2 weeks.

Tip: arrange the meat in a single layer without overlapping.

Nutrition Calories: 389 Fat 6.4 g Carbs 22.9 g Protein 49.3 g

Beer beef jerky

Preparation time: 6 hours and 10 minutes | Dehydration time: 5 hours

Servings: 2

Ingredients:

- 1 lb. Beef round, sliced
- 1/2 cup soy sauce
- 2 cloves garlic, minced
- 2 cups beer
- 1 tablespoon liquid smoke
- 1 tablespoon honey
- Pepper to taste

Direction:

1. Add the beef to a sealable plastic bag.
2. Combine the rest of the ingredients in a bowl.

3. Pour the mixture into the bag.

4. Seal and refrigerate for 6 hours.

5. Drain the marinade.

6. Place the beef in the cosori premium food dehydrator.

7. Dehydrate at 160 degrees f for 1 hour.

8. Reduce temperature to 150 degrees f and process for additional 4 hours.

9. Storage suggestions: store in a food container with lid for up to 2 weeks.

Tip: make sure beef is trimmed of fat before dehydrating.

Nutrition Calories: 389 Fat 6.4 g Carbs 22.9 g Protein 49.3 g

Fruit Recipes

Raw fig balls

Preparation time: 15 minutes | Dehydration time: 6 hours | Servings: 4

Ingredients:

- 1 cup raw almonds
- 10 dried figs
- 1/2 cup raisins
- 1/2 tsp. Almond extract
- 1/2 tsp. Vanilla extract
- 3/4 cup unsweetened coconut flakes

Direction:

1. Place the almonds in a food processor and pulse until they are ground. Add the figs, raisins and extracts and pulse until well combined.
2. Once the mixture is a dough-like consistency, roll into balls. Roll the balls in the coconut flakes.
3. Place balls on dehydrator trays and dry at 135 degrees for 4-6 hours.

Nutrition Calories:: 141, sodium: 4 mg, dietary fiber: 3 g, total fat: 9.7 g, total carbs: 12.3 g, protein: 2.8 g.

Spiced apple chips

Preparation time: 15 minutes | Dehydration time: 6 hours | Servings: 4

Ingredients:

- 3-4 ripe apples (any variety)
- 1 tbsp. Ground cinnamon
- 1/8 tsp. Either nutmeg, cloves, allspice, ginger or cardamom
- 1 tbsp. Sugar

Direction:

1. Slice the apple into thin rounds, between 1/8 – 1/4 inch thick. Peels can be removed or left intact. Remove core and seeds.
2. Toss sliced apples with the cinnamon, nutmeg, cloves and sugar.
3. Arrange in a single line in your dehydrator and set temperature to 135. Allow apples to dehydrate for 6-8 hours.

Nutrition Calories:: 36, sodium: 1 mg, dietary fiber: 2.7 g, total fat: 0.1 g, total carbs: 10.3 g, protein: 0.2 g.

☆ ☆ ☆ ☆ ☆

Spicy strawberry fruit leather

Preparation time: 15 minutes | Dehydration time: 6 hours | Servings: 4

Ingredients:

- 1 lb strawberries, hulled and chopped
- 1/3 cup granulated sugar
- 1 tbsp. Lemon juice
- 1 jalapeno or serrano pepper, seeds removed

Direction:

1. Puree strawberries, sugar, lemon juice and pepper.
2. Pour mixture onto fruit leather sheet of your dehydrator.
3. Spread puree evenly, about 1/8 inch thick, onto drying tray.
4. Set the temperature to 140 degrees. Dry for 6-8 hours, or touch center of leather to determine dryness.

Nutrition Calories:: 67, sodium: 0 mg, dietary fiber: 0 g, total fat: 0 g, total carbs: 17.9 g, protein: 0.1 g.

☆ ☆ ☆ ☆ ☆

Blackberry tuile

Preparation time: 10 minutes | Dehydration time: 3 hours | Servings: 4

Ingredients:

- 1 1/2 lb. Blackberries
- 2 tablespoons white sugar

Direction:

1. Process the blackberries and sugar in a blender.
2. Strain the mixture to remove the seeds.
3. Add the mixture to the blender.
4. Process on high speed.
5. Pour the fruit liquid into a fruit roll sheet.
6. Place these in the cosori premium food dehydrator.
7. Dehydrate at 165 degrees f for 3 hours.
8. Storage suggestions: store in a food container with lid, away from direct sunlight.

Tip: you can also slice the blackberries first and remove the seeds so you only have to blend it once.

Fruit leather

Preparation time: 30 minutes | Dehydration time: 8 hours | Servings: 4

Ingredients:

- 3 peaches, sliced
- 3 apricots, sliced
- 1 tablespoon sugar

Direction:

1. Put the peaches and apricots in a pot over medium low heat.
2. Sprinkle with sugar.

3. Mix well.
4. Cook for 10 minutes.
5. Let cool.
6. Transfer to a blender.
7. Blend on low speed until pureed.
8. Pour the mixture into a fruit roll sheet.
9. Place the roll sheet in the cosori premium food dehydrator.
10. Dehydrate at 165 degrees f or 8 hours.
11. Storage suggestions: arrange the solidified fruits on a baking tray and let it sit for a few minutes before storing in a food container.

Tip: you can also dehydrate for up to 12 hours to obtain drier results.

Vanilla-apricot slices

Preparation time: 15 minutes | Dehydration time: 6 hours | Servings: 4

Ingredients:

- 6-9 medium sized apricots, pitted
- 1 1/2 tsp. Honey
- 4 tbsp. Warm water
- Seeds from one vanilla bean, scraped out

Direction:

1. In a bowl, mix honey and vanilla seeds. Add the water and mix well. Combine until vanilla seeds are well separated.
2. Slice apricots into thin slices. Place apricot slices onto dehydrator tray and brush on a thin layer of vanilla mixture. It is not necessary for all the vanilla seeds to stick to the fruit.
3. Dehydrate for 9-12 hours at 135 degrees.

Nutrition Calories:: 17, sodium: 0 mg, dietary fiber: 0.5 g, total fat: 0.2 g, total carbs: 4.1 g, protein: 0.3 g.

Watermelon candy slices

Preparation time: 15 minutes | Dehydration time: 6 hours | Servings: 4

Ingredients:

- 1 watermelon
- Fleur de sel

Direction:

1. Cut the watermelon into slices and remove the rinds. Slices should be approximately 1/4 inch thick.
2. Lay watermelon slices on trays.
3. Sprinkle fleur de sel on top of the watermelon.
4. Place sheets in dehydrator at 135 degrees for 18 hours.

Nutrition Calories:: 9, sodium: 0 mg, dietary fiber: 0 g, total fat: 0 g, total carbs: 2.1 g, protein: 0.2 g.

Honey peaches with bourbon

Preparation time: 4 hours and 10 minutes | Dehydration time: 16 hours

Servings: 1

Ingredients:

- 1 peach, cored and sliced
- 1/4 cup honey
- 1/4 cup hot water
- 3 tablespoons bourbon

Direction:

1. Add the slices to a sealable plastic bag.

2. In a glass bowl, mix the honey and hot water.
3. Mix until the honey has been dissolved.
4. Pour in the bourbon.
5. Let cool.
6. Once cool, add this to the plastic bag.
7. Marinate for 4 hours.
8. Drain the marinade.
9. Add these to the cosori premium food dehydrator.
10. Dehydrate at 145 degrees f for 16 hours.
11. Storage suggestions: pack in a sealable plastic bag for up to 10 days.

Tip: you can also skip the bourbon and marinate in honey only.

Nutrition Calories: 389 Fat 6.4 g Carbs 22.9 g Protein 49.3 g

☆ ☆ ☆ ☆ ☆

Raspberry rolls

Preparation time: 10 minutes | Dehydration time: 5 hours | Servings: 4

Ingredients:

- 1 1/2 lb. Raspberries
- 2 tablespoons sugar

Direction:

1. Add the raspberries and sugars to a blender.
2. Blend until smooth.
3. Strain to remove the seeds.
4. Add the pureed raspberry back to the blender. 5. Blend until the mixture has turned into liquid.
5. Add the liquid to a fruit roll sheet.
6. Place these in the cosori premium food dehydrator.
7. Dehydrate at 165 degrees f for 5 hours.
8. Storage suggestions: store in a glass jar with lid in a cool dry

place.

Tip: you can also use strawberries or blueberries to make this recipe.

Nutrition Calories: 389 Fat 6.4 g Carbs 22.9 g Protein 49.3 g

Dried apple chips with cinnamon

Preparation time: 15 hours | Dehydration time: 6 hours | Servings: 2

Ingredients:

- 2 apples, sliced
- 1 tablespoon lemon juice
- 2 teaspoons cinnamon powder

Direction:

1. Drizzle the apple slices with lemon juice.
2. Arrange the apple slices in the cosori premium food dehydrator.
3. Process at 135 degrees f for 6 hours.
4. Sprinkle with the cinnamon before serving.
5. Storage suggestions: store in a glass jar with lid.

Tip: you can also keep the apple peel if you like but scrub the peel first with apple cider vinegar before processing.

Nutrition Calories: 389 Fat 6.4 g Carbs 22.9 g Protein 49.3 g

Candied pumpkin

Preparation time: 15 minutes | Dehydration time: 8 hours | Servings: 2

Ingredients:

- 1 cup coconut milk

- 2 cups applesauce
- 2 cups pumpkin puree
- 1/4 cup honey
- 1/2 teaspoon ground allspice
- 1/2 teaspoon ground nutmeg
- 1 teaspoon ground cinnamon
- 1/4 cup coconut flakes
- 2 tablespoons dried cranberries, chopped

Direction:

1. Combine all the ingredients in a bowl.
2. Spread the mixture in the fruit leather sheet of your cosori premium food dehydrator.
3. Dehydrate at 135 degrees f for 8 hours.
4. Storage suggestions: slice the fruit leather before storing in a food container with lid.

Tip: grease the fruit leather sheet with a little bit of oil before processing.

Nutrition Calories: 163 Fat 12.3 g Carbs 6.7 g Protein 6.6 g

Orange fruit leather

Preparation time: 10 minutes | Dehydration time: 6 hours | Servings: 4

Ingredients:

- 1 cup applesauce
- 1 cup orange juice concentrate
- 32 oz. Vanilla yogurt

Direction:

1. Add all the ingredients in your blender.
2. Pulse until smooth.

3. Spread the mixture onto the roll sheet.
4. Dry at 135 degrees f for 6 hours.
5. Storage suggestions: store in an airtight food container for up to 2 weeks.

Tip: grease the roll sheet with a little olive oil before processing.

Nutrition Calories: 163 Fat 12.3 g Carbs 6.7 g Protein 6.6 g

Dried lemon

Preparation time: 5 minutes | Dehydration time: 6 hours | Servings: 2

Ingredients:

- 2 lemons, sliced

Direction:

1. Arrange the lemon slices in the cosori premium food dehydrator.
2. Dry the lemon at 125 degrees f for 6 hours.
3. Storage suggestions: store in an airtight container.

Tip: drizzle with honey before drying if you like them a little sweeter.

Dried papaya cubes

Preparation time: 10 minutes | Dehydration time: 12 hours | Servings: 4

Ingredients:

- 2 papaya, diced

Direction:

1. Add the diced papaya to the cosori premium food dehydrator.

2. Process at 135 degrees f for 12 hours.
3. Storage suggestions: store in an airtight jar.

Tip: you can also sprinkle with sugar before dehydrating.

Nutrition Calories: 11 protein: 0.04 g fat: 0.03g carbs: 2.85 g

☆ ☆ ☆ ☆ ☆

Dried kiwi

Preparation time: 15 minutes | Dehydration time: 12 hours | Servings: 2

Ingredients:

- 2 kiwis, peeled and sliced thinly

Direction:

1. Place the kiwi slices in the cosori premium food dehydrator.
2. Dry at 135 degrees f for 12 hours.
3. Storage suggestions: store in a glass jar with lid. Place the jar in a cool dry place.

Tip: kiwi slices should be at least 6mm thick.

Nutrition Calories: 11 protein: 0.04 g fat: 0.03g carbs: 2.85 g

☆ ☆ ☆ ☆ ☆

Cinnamon apple chips

Preparation time: 10 minutes | Dehydration time: 12 hours | Servings: 4

Ingredients:

- 2 apples, sliced thinly
- 1 tablespoon white sugar
- 1 tablespoon lemon juice
- 1/4 teaspoon nutmeg

- 1/2 teaspoon vanilla extract
- 1 teaspoon ground cinnamon

Direction:

1. Combine all the ingredients in a bowl.
2. Coat the apples slices evenly with the mixture.
3. Arrange the apple slices in the cosori premium food dehydrator.
4. Dehydrate at 145 degrees f for 6 hours.
5. Storage suggestions: store in a glass jar with lid.

Tip: apple slices should be at least 1/4 inch thick.

☆ ☆ ☆ ☆ ☆

Plum & grape fruit leather

Preparation time: 20 minutes | Dehydration time: 12 hours | Servings: 4

Ingredients:

- 2 cups red grapes (seedless)
- 5 plums, sliced
- 2 tablespoons sugar

Direction:

1. Put all the ingredients in a pot over medium low heat.
2. Cook for 15 minutes.
3. Transfer the mixture to a blender.
4. Blend until smooth.
5. Pour the mixture into a fruit roll sheet.
6. Place in the cosori premium food dehydrator.
7. Process at 165 degrees f for 12 hours.
8. Storage suggestions: dry the fruit leather on a tray after dehydrating and before storing.

Tip: you can also process for 8 hours only.

☆ ☆ ☆ ☆ ☆

Berry fruit leather

Preparation time: 10 minutes | Dehydration time: 6 hours | Servings: 4

Ingredients:

- 1 lb. Strawberries
- 1/2 cup raspberries
- 1 teaspoon vanilla extract

Direction:

1. Process all the ingredients in a blender.
2. Pulse until smooth.
3. Strain to remove seeds.
4. Put the mixture back to the blender.
5. Pulse until liquified.
6. Pour the fruit puree into a fruit roll sheet and place in the cosori premium food dehydrator.
7. Dehydrate at 165 degrees f for 6 hours.
8. Storage suggestions: sprinkle with white sugar before storing in a glass jar.

Tip: you can also use other berries for this recipe.

☆ ☆ ☆ ☆ ☆

Dried strawberries

Preparation time: 10 minutes | Dehydration time: 8 hours | Servings: 4

Ingredients:

- 1 lb. Strawberries, sliced

Direction:

1. Place the strawberry slices in the cosori premium food

dehydrator.

2. Process at 135 degrees f for 8 hours.
3. Storage suggestions: keep in a glass jar with lid.

Tip: hull and slice the strawberries before dehydrating them. Slices should be 1/8 inch thick.

Hazelnut banana leather

Preparation time: 5 minutes | Dehydration time: 3 hours | Servings: 2

Ingredients:

- 2 bananas, sliced
- Chocolate hazelnut spread

Direction:

1. Combine the bananas and chocolate hazelnut spread in your food processor.
2. Pulse until smooth.
3. Form round shapes of about ¼ inch thick on parchment paper.
4. Transfer to the cosori premium food dehydrator.
5. Process at 125 degrees f for 4 hours.
6. Storage suggestions: store in a glass jar with lid. Place jar in a cool dry place.

Tip: the treats should no longer be sticky when touched.

Apple fruit leather

Preparation time: 10 minutes | Dehydration time: 6 hours | Servings: 2

Ingredients:

- 2 cups applesauce

- 2 cups sweet potatoes, cooked and mashed
- 1/4 cup honey
- 1 teaspoon cinnamon
- Salt to taste

Direction:

1. Add all the ingredients to a blender.
2. Pulse until smooth.
3. Add the mixture to fruit roll sheets and place in the cosori premium food dehydrator.
4. Dry at 100 degrees f for 6 hours.
5. Storage suggestions: store apple leather in a sealable plastic bag.

Tip: you can also add a little lemon juice to the mixture to balance the flavor.

Peanut butter & banana leather

Preparation time: 5 minutes | Dehydration time: 4 hours | Servings: 2

Ingredients:

- 2 bananas, sliced
- 2 tablespoons peanut butter

Direction:

1. Process bananas and peanut butter in a food processor for 1 minute.
2. Spread a layer of the mixture onto the dehydrator sheet.
3. Dry at 135 degrees f for 4 hours.
4. Storage suggestions: slice the leather before storing.

Tip: you can also add melted chocolate into the mixture if you like.

Sweet and sour cranberries

Preparation time: 15 minutes | Dehydration time: 6 hours | Servings: 4

Ingredients:

- 12 oz. Cranberries
- 1/4 cup corn syrup (or sugar)
- Zest of one orange and one lime

Direction:

1. Place cranberries in a bowl and pour boiling water over them until the skins crack. Drain.
2. Toss the berries with corn syrup or sugar and zests. Place berries on cooking sheet and freeze for 2 hours to promote faster drying.
3. Assemble berries on a mesh sheet in the dehydrator and dry at 135 degrees for 12-16 hours or until chewy.

Nutrition Calories:: 41, sodium: 0 mg, dietary fiber: 0.6 g, total fat: 0 g, total carbs: 10.2 g, protein: 0 g.

Sweet "caramel apples"

Preparation time: 15 minutes | Dehydration time: 6 hours | Servings: 4

Ingredients:

- 3-4 granny smith apples
- 1/2 cup store-bought caramel sauce

Direction:

1. Slice the apple into thin rounds, between 1/8-1/4 inch thick. Peels can be removed or left intact. Remove core and seeds.
2. Use a pastry brush to spread a small amount of caramel onto each apple round.

3. Arrange in a single line in your dehydrator and set temperature to 135 degrees. Allow apples to dehydrate for 10-12 hours.

Nutrition Calories:: 41, sodium: 45 mg, dietary fiber: 0 g, total fat: 0 g, total carbs: 10.6 g, protein: 0.2 g.

Sweet potato- cinnamon leather

Preparation time: 15 minutes | Dehydration time: 6 hours | Servings: 4

Ingredients:

- 3 medium sweet potatoes
- 1/2 tsp. Cinnamon
- 1/8 tsp. Ground ginger

Direction:

1. Preheat oven to 400 degrees and place sweet potatoes in a baking dish. Cover and bake 35-45 minutes, or until soft.
2. Peel skins and put potatoes in food processor with cinnamon and ginger. Puree until smooth.
3. Pour mixture onto dehydrator trays and spread to 1/4 inch thickness. Dehydrate at 135 degree for 86 hours.

Nutrition Calories:: 33, sodium: 3 mg, dietary fiber: 1.2 g, total fat: 0.1 g, total carbs: 7.9 g, protein: 0.4 g

Tangy dried mangos

Preparation time: 15 minutes | Dehydration time: 6 hours | Servings: 4

Ingredients:

- 4-5 ripe mangoes

- 1 tbsp. Honey
- 1/4 cup lime juice
- Pinch of salt

Direction:

1. Peel and slice mangoes into thin, even strips.
2. Dissolve honey in lemon juice. Mix well and add salt.
3. Dip mango slices into honey mixture. Shake off excess.
4. Arrange in a single line in your dehydrator and set temperature to 135 degrees. Allow mangoes to dehydrate for 8-9 hours.

Nutrition Calories:: 21, sodium: 1 mg, dietary fiber: 0.5 g, total fat: 0.1 g, total carbs: 5.3 g, protein: 0.1 g.

Tropical pineapple crisps

Preparation time: 15 minutes | Dehydration time: 6 hours | Servings: 4

Ingredients:

- 1 ripe pineapple
- Coconut oil
- 1/2 cup sweetened coconut flakes
- Sea salt to taste

Direction:

1. Peel and core the pineapple. Slice into thin, uniform rounds about 1/2 inch thick.
2. Using a pastry brush, spread a thin layer of coconut oil on each pineapple slice. Sprinkle with coconut flakes and a small amount of sea salt.
3. Arrange in a single line in your dehydrator and set temperature to 135 degrees. Allow pineapple to dehydrate for 12-16 hours, flipping the slices halfway through for even dryness.

Nutrition Calories:: 51, sodium: 21 mg, dietary fiber: 0.8 g, total fat: 2.6 g, total carbs: 6.1 g, protein: 0.7 g.

Grains, Nuts and Seeds Recipes

Almond cranberry cookies

Preparation time: 15 minutes | Dehydration time: 6 hours | Servings: 4

Ingredients:

- Wet pulp from almond milk
- 1 banana
- 2 tbsp. Coconut oil
- 3/4 cup shredded coconut flakes
- 1/2 cup dried cranberries
- 1 tbsp. Honey
- 1/2 cup almonds, coarsely chopped

Direction:

1. Place almond pulp, banana and coconut oil in food processor.
2. Mix remainder of ingredients and add to the almond pulp mixture.
3. Place a small scoop of dough on dehydrator sheets and flatten into a cookie.
4. Set temperature to 105 degrees and dehydrate for 6 hours or more.
5. Set temperature to 105 degrees and dehydrate for 6 hours or more.

Nutrition Calories:: 91, sodium: 2 mg, dietary fiber: 2.3 g, total fat: 7.6 g, total carbs: 4.8 g, protein: 2 g.

Apple and nut "raw" cereal

Preparation time: 15 minutes | Dehydration time: 6 hours |Servings: 4

Ingredients:

- 1 apple, peeled, cored and diced

- 1 cup sprouted wheat berries
- 1/2 cup flax seeds, ground
- 1/2 cup diced raw walnuts
- 1/2 cup millet flour
- 1 cup sunflower seeds
- 1 tsp. Cinnamon
- 1/4 tsp. Salt
- 1/4 cup coconut oil, melted
- 1/4 cup maple syrup
- 3 tbsp. Apple juice

Direction:

1. Combine apple, wheat berries, flax seeds, walnuts, flour, seeds, cinnamon and salt.
2. Blend coconut oil, maple syrup and apple juice with a whisk.
3. Add dry ingredients to wet ingredients and stir thoroughly.
4. Dehydrate at 115 degrees for 18-24 hours. When crispy, break into large pieces.

Nutrition Calories:: 120, sodium: 19 mg, dietary fiber: 2.5 g, total fat: 7.6 g, total carbs: 9.9 g, protein: 4.2 g.

Apple cinnamon graham cookies

Preparation time: 15 minutes | Dehydration time: 6 hours | Servings: 4

Ingredients:

- 1 cup cashews, soaked for 1 hour
- 1 cup pecans, soaked for 1 hour
- 6 cups ground almonds
- 2 apples, peeled, cored and chopped
- 1 pear, peeled, cored and chopped
- 1 cup almond butter

- 1 1/2 cups flax seed
- 1/2 cup honey
- 1 tbsp. Cinnamon
- 1/2 tsp. Nutmeg
- Pinch of salt

Direction:

1. After nuts have been soaked, drain and rinse them.
2. Pulse cashews and pecans in food processor until small crumbs form. Add the ground almonds and place in a bowl.
3. In the food processor, combine apples, pear, almond butter, flax seed, honey, cinnamon, nutmeg and salt. Add the ground nuts.
4. Spread mixture on dehydrator trays, about 1/4 inch thick, to the edges.
5. Dehydrate 6-8 hours at 115 degrees. Flip over and cut into squares. Continue dehydrating for 6-8 hours or until crunchy.

Nutrition Calories:: 160, sodium: 2 mg, dietary fiber: 3.5 g, total fat: 13.3 g, total carbs: 6.8 g, protein: 5.1 g.

☆ ☆ ☆ ☆ ☆

Asian-inspired nuts

Preparation time: 15 minutes | Dehydration time: 6 hours | Servings: 4

Ingredients:

- 16 ounce jar of roasted peanuts
- 1/3 cup soy sauce
- 1/4 cup water
- 1 1/2 tsp. Sesame oil
- 1/2 tsp. Five spice powder
- 1/4 tsp. Ground ginger

Direction:

1. Place nuts in a bowl. Combine all other ingredients and whisk together.
2. Pour over nuts. Marinate nuts at least 8 hours or overnight.
3. Drain liquid and place nuts on dehydrator tray. Dehydrate for 5 hours at 135 degrees.

Nutrition Calories:: 152, sodium: 5 mg, dietary fiber: 2.3 g, total fat: 13.1 g, total carbs: 4.4 g, protein: 6.9 g.

Banana breakfast crepes

Preparation time: 15 minutes | Dehydration time: 6 hours | Servings: 4

Ingredients:

- 2 medium size ripe bananas
- 1 tsp. Ground flax seed
- 1 tsp. Almond meal
- 1 tsp. Almond milk
- Dash of cinnamon

Direction:

1. Place all ingredients in a food processor and blend into a liquid.
2. Line 2 dehydrator sheets and pour mixture onto them. Liquid should only be about 1/8 inches in thickness. Spread with a spatula.
3. Dehydrate at 115 degrees for 3 hours. Crepes should be totally smooth. Do not remove crepes early or they will not hold their shape. Cut into crepe-sized circles.

Nutrition Calories:: 48, sodium: 1 mg, dietary fiber: 1.6 g, total fat: 2 g, total carbs: 6.6 g, protein: 1.2 g.

★ ☆ ★ ☆ ★

Basic "soaked nuts"

Preparation time: 15 minutes | Dehydration time: 6 hours | Servings: 4

Ingredients:

- Nuts, in any quantity and variety
- Sea salt, approximately
- 1 tbsp. Per every 4 cups of nuts
- Filtered water (to cover the nuts)

Direction:

1. Combine nuts, sea salt and water in a glass bowl. Cover with a lid or plate and place in a warm location for 12 hours.
2. Remove lid and rinse nuts in a colander.
3. Spread nuts in a single layer on dehydrator trays for 12-24 hours at 105-150 degrees.

★ ☆ ★ ☆ ★

Flax seed crackers

Preparation time: 15 minutes | Dehydration time: 6 hours | Servings: 4

Ingredients:

- 2 cups flaxseeds
- 2 cups water
- 1/4 cup low sodium soy sauce
- 2 tbsp. Sesame seeds
- Sea salt and black pepper, to taste
- 1 1/2 tbsp. Fresh lime juice

Direction:

1. Cover flax seeds with water and soak for 1-2 hours. Mixture

should be gooey, but not too thin. Add more water to achieve this texture.

2. Stir in the remainder of the ingredients.
3. Spread the mixture about 1/8 inch thick on dehydrator sheets.
4. Set the temperature to 105-115 degrees and dehydrate 4-6 hours. Flip over mixture and dehydrate another 4-6 hours. Break crackers into large pieces after dehydrating.

Nutrition Calories:: 133, sodium: 7 mg, dietary fiber: 6.5 g, total fat: 8.2 g, total carbs: 7.1 g, protein: 4.6 g.

Fruit n' nut balls

Preparation time: 15 minutes | Dehydration time: 6 hours | Servings: 4

Ingredients:

- 1/2 cup dried dates
- 1/2 cup figs
- 1/2 cup dried cherries
- 1/2 cup dried apricots
- 1/2 cup dried cranberries
- 1 cup crushed pecans
- 1 cup crushed almonds
- 3 tsp. Coconut oil, melted
- 1 cup flaked coconut

Direction:

1. Finely process dates, figs, cherries, apricots and cranberries in a food processor. Mix with nuts and coconut oil in a bowl.
2. Shape into 1" balls and roll balls in coconut.
3. Place in dehydrator at 135 degrees for 6 hours.

Nutrition Calories:: 102, sodium: 2 mg, dietary fiber: 2.3 g, total fat:

8.4 g, total carbs: 6.9 g, protein: 2 g.

☆ ☆ ☆ ☆ ☆

Fruit & nut clusters

Preparation time: 15 minutes | Dehydration time: 6 hours | Servings: 4

Ingredients:

- 1/2 cup cashew butter
- 1/2 cup maple syrup
- 1 1/2 tsp. Cinnamon
- 1 tsp. Salt
- 1 tsp. Vanilla extract
- 8 dates, pitted
- 2 cups cashews
- 1 cup pecans
- 1 cup dried cranberries
- 1 cup dried blueberries
- 1 cup rolled oats, raw

Direction:

1. In a food processor, combine cashew butter, maple syrup, cinnamon, salt, vanilla extract and dates. Pulse until the mixture is smooth.
2. In a bowl, combine cashews, pecans, dried fruits and oats. Pour liquid mixture on top and toss to coat.
3. Pour batter onto dehydrator sheets and dehydrate for 1 hour at 145 degrees. Reduce temperature to 115 degrees and continue dehydrating for up to 24 hours.

Nutrition Calories:: 110, sodium: 37 mg, dietary fiber: 1.6 g, total fat: 7.9 g, total carbs: 9.2 g, protein: 2.8 g.

☆ ☆ ☆ ☆ ☆

Graham crackers"

Preparation time: 15 minutes | Dehydration time: 6 hours | Servings: 4

Ingredients:

- 4 cups almond flour
- 1 cup oat flour
- 1/2 cup flax seeds
- 1/2 cup almond milk
- 1 cup maple syrup
- 1 tbsp. Vanilla
- 1 tbsp. Cinnamon

Direction:

1. Pulse all ingredients in the food processor.
2. Spread onto dehydrator trays. Make sure graham cracker mixture is about 1/8 inch thick.
3. Dehydrate at 115 degrees for 4 hours.
4. Cut into squares and then flip and dehydrate for 6 more hours.

Nutrition Calories:: 142, sodium: 7 mg, dietary fiber: 3.2 g, total fat: 10.2 g, total carbs: 9.6 g, protein: 5 g.

Hazelnut lemon crackers

Preparation time: 15 minutes | Dehydration time: 7 hours | Servings: 4

Ingredients:

- 1/2 cup chia seeds
- 1 cup water
- 3 cups hazelnuts, soaked overnight, skins removed
- 1 1/2 tbsp. Lemon zest
- 1 tbsp. Maple syrup

- 1/2 tsp. Sea salt
- Black pepper to taste

Direction:

1. Mix chia seeds in 1 cup water and allow to soften.
2. Remove soaked hazelnuts and drain them. Place hazelnuts in food processor and grind until fine.
3. Pour ground nuts into a bowl and combine with chia seeds, lemon zest, maple syrup, salt and pepper.
4. Spread onto dehydrator trays. Use a spatula to flatten dough to approximately 1/4 inch thick. Dehydrate at 145 degrees for 1 hour. Decrease heat to 115 and continue to dehydrate for 8 hours.

Nutrition Calories:: 169, sodium: 31 mg, dietary fiber: 3.7 g, total fat: 15.6 g, total carbs: 5.5 g, protein: 4.4 g.

Macadamia-sage crackers

Preparation time: 15 minutes | Dehydration time: 6 hours | Servings: 4

Ingredients:

- 2 cups macadamia nuts
- 2 cups chia or flax seeds
- 1 1/2 tbsp. Fresh sage, crushed
- Sea salt and white pepper to taste
- 3 cups water
- 1/2 cup olive oil

Direction:

1. Place macadamia nuts and flax seeds into a food processor and grind into a flour. Add sage, salt and pepper. Process until you have a fine texture.

2. In a large bowl, add water to nut and seed mix and stir until thick. Don't pour all the water at once. Add small amounts until a soft dough forms.
3. Spread onto dehydrator sheets. Drizzle with olive oil and sprinkle additional sea salt.
4. Dehydrate at 110 degrees for 4 hours. Score the crackers, flip them over and dehydrate another 8 hours.

Nutrition Calories:: 176, sodium: 1 mg, dietary fiber: 6.4 g, total fat: 15.1 g, total carbs: 7.2 g, protein: 4.2 g.

Mint-scented chocolate chip cookies

Preparation time: 15 minutes | Dehydration time: 6 hours | Servings: 4

Ingredients:

- 1 1/2 cups almond meal
- 1 1/2 cups ground pecans
- 1 cup cocoa powder
- 1/4 cup cacao nibs
- 1/2 cup maple syrup
- 3 tbsp. Coconut oil
- 1 tsp. Peppermint extract
- 1 tsp. Vanilla extract
- 1 tbsp. Almond milk
- 1/2 tsp. Salt

Direction:

1. Place all ingredients in food processor and pulse until combined. Ingredients should form a cohesive dough.
2. Roll out dough to about 1/4 inch thickness.
3. Cut out circles using a small glass. Alternatively, skip this process, roll dough into balls and flatten into disks.

4. Dehydrate for 24 hours at 115 degrees.

Nutrition Calories:: 140, sodium: 25 mg, dietary fiber: 4.7 g, total fat: 12.1 g, total carbs: 8.8 g, protein: 4.3 g.

Orange-scented granola with dried blueberries

Preparation time: 15 minutes | Dehydration time: 6 hours | Servings: 4

Ingredients:

- 2 cups raw buckwheat or oat groats
- 1 cup dates, pitted
- 1 cup freshly squeezed orange juice
- 1 orange, juiced
- 1 tsp. Almond extract
- 1 tsp. Lemon juice
- 1/2 cup dried blueberries

Direction:

1. Soak the groats in water and drain after about 1 hour. Rinse well and drain again. Transfer them to a small bowl.
2. In a food processor, pulse all other ingredients except dried blueberries until a paste forms. Blend this mixture with the groats. Mix thoroughly.
3. Spread mixture on dehydrator sheets. Dehydrate for 12 hours at 115 degrees and flip over. Dehydrate for another 12-15 hours until granola is crispy.
4. After dehydrated, crumble granola into bite size pieces and add dried blueberries.

Nutrition Calories:: 85, sodium: 0 mg, dietary fiber: 2 g, total fat: 0.7 g, total carbs: 17.4 g, protein: 2.2 g.

☆ ☆ ☆ ☆ ☆

Parmesan black pepper flax crackers

Preparation time: 15 minutes | Dehydration time: 6 hours | Servings: 4

Ingredients:

- 1 cup flax seeds
- 1 cup water
- 1/4 cup parmesan cheese
- 1/2 tbsp. Black pepper
- 1 clove garlic
- 1 tsp. Flaky sea salt

Direction:

1. Stir all ingredients in a large bowl until it forms a gelatinous dough.
2. Spread onto dehydrator sheets so that mixture is about 1/4 inch thick. Slice the dough into squares.
3. Set temperature to 145 degrees and dehydrate for 30-45 minutes. Reduce temperature to 115 degrees and after 6 hours, flip the crackers.
4. Continue dehydrating for 12-18 hours. Crackers should be crispy when ready.

Nutrition Calories:: 131, sodium: 214 mg, dietary fiber: 6.4 g, total fat: 7.8 g, total carbs: 7.1 g, protein: 5.2 g.

☆ ☆ ☆ ☆ ☆

Pepita crackers

Preparation time: 15 minutes | Dehydration time: 6 hours | Servings: 4

Ingredients:

- 2 1/2 cups sprouted quinoa

- 3/4 cup chia seeds, finely ground
- 1/4 cup low sodium soy sauce
- 2 cloves garlic
- 1 tsp. Onion powder
- 1/2 tsp. Salt
- 1/2 cup pepitas

Direction:

1. Process quinoa until finely ground. Add all the other ingredients except pepitas and pulse until well combined.
2. Spread mixture on dehydrator sheets. Sprinkle pepitas on top and press down to adhere to mixture.
3. Cut into squares. Dehydrate for 8-12 hours at 140 degrees or until crunchy.

Nutrition Calories:: 107, sodium: 2 mg, dietary fiber: 3.3 g, total fat: 4.3 g, total carbs: 14.9 g, protein: 4.5 g.

Raw cheesy thyme crackers

Preparation time: 15 minutes | Dehydration time: 6 hours | Servings: 4

Ingredients:

- 2 cups almonds, soaked overnight and dried
- 4 tbsp. Ground chia seeds
- 4 tbsp. Nutritional yeast
- 2 1/2 tbsp. Fresh thyme, chopped
- 1/2 tsp. Salt

Direction:

1. Soak chia seeds in 1/2 cup of water for 30 minutes. Drain.
2. Place almonds, chia seeds, nutritional yeast, thyme and salt in a food processor. Pulse several times.

3. Add a few drops of water while motor is running until mixture becomes spreadable.

4. Spread mixture onto dehydrator sheets and set temperature to 115 degrees. Dehydrate for 4-6 hours. Flip over and cut into cracker shapes. Dehydrate another 8 hours.

Nutrition Calories:: 132, sodium: 37 mg, dietary fiber: 4.5 g, total fat: 10.4 g, total carbs: 7.2 g, protein: 5.5 g.

"Raw" granola

Preparation time: 15 minutes | Dehydration time: 6 hours | Servings: 4

Ingredients:

- 3 cups rolled oats
- 1/4 cup oat bran
- 1 cup raw pumpkin seeds
- 1 cup raw sunflower seeds
- 1 cup coconut
- 1 cup walnuts, pecans or almonds
- 1/2 cup honey
- 1/2 cup coconut oil, melted
- 1/2 cup water
- 1 tsp. Cinnamon
- 1/4 tsp. Nutmeg

Direction:

1. Mix together honey, oil and water. Add all the remaining ingredients.
2. Spread mixture onto dehydrator sheets and smooth to create a thin layer.
3. Dehydrate for 18 hours at 105-115 degrees.

Nutrition Calories:: 131, sodium: 7 mg, dietary fiber: 2.3 g, total fat:

7.8 g, total carbs: 12.1 g, protein: 4.7 g.

Savory onion and garlic crisps

Preparation time: 15 minutes | Dehydration time: 6 hours | Servings: 4

Ingredients:

- 1 vidalia onion, peeled and halved
- 2 cloves garlic, peeled and ground
- 1 cup ground flax seeds
- 1 cup ground chia seeds
- 1 1/2 cups ground sunflower seeds
- 1/2 cup low sodium soy sauce
- 1/2 cup extra virgin olive oil
- 1/2 tsp. White pepper

Direction:

1. Place onions and garlic in food processor and process roughly, but do not create a paste.
2. Transfer to a mixing bowl and add all other ingredients. Mix until combined.
3. Spread mixture on dehydrator sheet and dehydrate at 100 degrees for 24-36 hours.
4. After dehydrating, cut into large squares.

Nutrition Calories:: 116, sodium: 4 mg, dietary fiber: 7.7 g, total fat: 8.1 g, total carbs: 8.9 g, protein: 4.9

Savory trail mix

Preparation time: 15 minutes | Dehydration time: 6 hours | Servings: 4

Ingredients:

- 1 cup raw almonds, soaked overnight and dried
- 1 cup raw pumpkin seeds, soaked overnight and dried
- 1 cup raw sunflower seeds, soaked overnight and dried
- 3 tbsp. Low sodium soy sauce
- 3 tbsp. Olive oil
- 1 tsp. Garlic powder
- 2 tsp. Onion powder
- 1/2 tsp. Celery salt
- Pinch of cayenne pepper

Direction:

1. Combine soy sauce, olive oil and seasonings. Pour onto nuts and seeds and stir until they are well coated.
2. Spread mixture onto dehydrator tray using mesh sheets.
3. Dehydrate for 18 hours at 105-115 degrees.

Nutrition Calories:: 120, sodium: 19 mg, dietary fiber: 2.5 g, total fat: 7.6 g, total carbs: 9.9 g, protein: 4.2 g.

Seasoned sunflower seeds

Preparation time: 15 minutes | Dehydration time: 6 hours | Servings: 4

Ingredients:

- 2 tbsp. Olive oil
- 1 tbsp. Soy sauce
- 1/2 tsp. Garlic powder
- 1/2 tsp. Onion powder

- 1/2 tsp. Celery salt
- 1/4 tsp. Crushed red pepper flakes
- 2 cups shelled sunflower seeds, raw

Direction:

1. Soak sunflower seeds overnight. Rinse and dry thoroughly.
2. Mix together the olive oil, soy sauce and seasonings. Toss seeds in the mixture until they are well coated.
3. Place on a dehydrator tray and dehydrate for 12-18 hours at 105-115 degrees.

Nutrition Calories:: 140, sodium: 3 mg, dietary fiber: 2.1 g, total fat: 12.3 g, total carbs: 5 g, protein: 5 g.

www.ingramcontent.com/pod-product-compliance
Lightning Source LLC
Chambersburg PA
CBHW060933050726